Honor
Lost

Honor
Lost

Love and Death in Modern-Day Jordan

❧❧

Norma Khouri

ATRIA BOOKS

NEW YORK   LONDON   TORONTO   SYDNEY   SINGAPORE

ATRIA BOOKS
1230 Avenue of the Americas
New York, New York 10020

ISBN: 0-7434-4878-2

First Atria Books hardcover printing February 2003

10 9 8 7 6 5 4 3 2 1

ATRIA BOOKS is a trademark of Simon & Schuster, Inc.

For information regarding special discounts for bulk purchases,
please contact Simon & Schuster Special Sales at 1-800-456-6798 or
business@simonandschuster.com

Printed in the U.S.A.

ACKNOWLEDGMENTS

First and foremost I would like to thank God for giving me the ability to put this into words, and for making sure it reached the right hands. Second, I would like to thank Christy Fletcher, Whitney Lee, and Greer Hendricks without whose friendship, dedication, honesty, guidance, and professionalism this book would not exist today. Also I would like to thank the many wonderful people in the literary world who have come together on this project in one way or another for their support, guidance and encouragement: Liza, Moira, Sarah, Brenda, Annabel, Arabella, Suzanne, Patrick, Fiona, Elana, and the many, many, others involved. Kevin, who reminded me to "go on again with fresh courage," and J.T. for the moral support.

Honor
Lost

PROLOGUE

Jordan is a place where men in sand-colored business suits hold cell phones to one ear and, in the other, hear the whispers of harsh and ancient laws blowing in from the desert. It is a place where a worldly young queen argues eloquently on CNN for human rights, while a father in a middle-class suburb slits his daughter's throat for committing the most innocent breach of old Bedouin codes of honor.

It is a place of paradox and double standards for men and women, for liberated and conservative. Modern on the surface, it is an unforgiving desert whose oases have blossomed into cities. But the desert continues to blow in. Streets are parched and stripped of flowers, trees, or greenery—except for a rare grapevine in private patios, and new steel and glass corporate towers reflect the tawny colors of the dunes. In their shadow, cafés are full of high-tech chatter, and young men in Jordan's requisite tan suit coat and Levi's rub elbows with elders in *dishdashay*, the ankle-length dress shirt that is a vestige of the desert. Young women in veils view with envy the "modern" girls sipping espresso, smoking, slim crossed legs exposed to the knee.

Unlike the Jordan River, no longer strong enough to flow down

I

to Amman, the desert drifts up to the city's boundaries. Like the sand that coats the streets after a windstorm, the Bedouin code is always encroaching on its urban streets. It permeates my family's neighborhood in Amman, dense-packed and tight-knit as a nomadic camp and filled with descendants of the original tribes. Its fierce and primitive code is always nagging at men's instincts, reminding them that under the Westernizing veneer, they are all still Arabs. For most women, Jordan is a stifling prison tense with the risk of death at the hands of loved ones. It is my home. I love its stark beauty, its sweep of history. And yet it may never be safe for me to return.

๛๏๛

But let me set the stage for this story by giving some sense of my strange, conflicted nation. Bordered by Saudi Arabia, Egypt, Israel, Lebanon, Syria, Iraq, and Kuwait, the Hashemite Kingdom of Jordan sits at the beating geographic heart of the Arab world. A constitutional monarchy with King Abdullah Bin Hussein and Queen Rania presenting our modern face to the world, it is a small, predominantly Muslim country—less than 5 million of its population is Muslim, though Christians live side by side. Its capital, Amman, is home to a third of the nation's people, as well as to a horde of historical, cultural, and social riches. Beyond Amman, the Roman Pillars of Jerash, the Nabateen temples of Petra carved from canyons of pink stone that glow with magical light as the sun strikes at dawn and sunset, the Byzantine mosaics of Madaba, Mount Nebo, and Wadi Kharrar, the baptismal site of Christ, continue to lure travelers and pilgrims.

Jordan swaggers with pride at being a modern, technologically advanced, and rapidly democratizing nation (or so it would like the world to believe). But the process is often as awkward and outdated as the 1970s American suits men still wear to the office. Amman did progress dramatically in the final decade of the twentieth century. New hotels and banks sprang up on virtually every city street. Computers equipped with the latest technology brought their quiet power to offices and homes everywhere, linking Jordanians to the larger world. Cell phones, pagers, and portable faxes are now as common as a pair of sunglasses. The government has spent millions annually to attract foreign investors, improve commerce, and increase tourism.

Yet a few hours' drive from this modern metropolis is a world that existed before Christ. Spend a day in Wadi Rum, exploring the Nabateen and Thamudic cave drawings with the Bedouins—barter for their jangling jewelry or share tea in their goat-hair tents, and you'll feel as if you've gone back in time. Jordan is one of a very few countries where the present and past live in tense and dynamic coexistence. It is a country that unfurls banners of welcome to the future, yet holds tenaciously to its ancient roots and traditions.

For Jordanian women progress has been slower coming than for men. We are now allowed to study any subject we want as long as the men in our families—i.e., our fathers, brothers, or, if married, husbands—give us their permission. And, compared to women in most Muslim countries, particularly Saudi Arabia, women in Jordan have certain freedoms and privileges—access to a full education, the right to drive cars, and, as of 1989, the right to vote, provided, of course, that the male heads of our households approve. Yes, Jordan can claim many women doctors, but their numbers reveal a dark side for women: they are so fully segregated from men that a woman dare not be seen by a male doctor. And the women doctors come mostly from the very wealthy and modern families, families that can afford to live through the gossip or rumors that arise.

In a country that boasts of its modernity, a woman's decisions are still made by men. A man must authorize everything in her life, from the person she marries to her wardrobe. It's a male-dominated world with very limited and controlled "freedoms" for women.

So while men celebrate their country's progress, women still pray that their silent cries will be heard. Even for the women who, on the street, look liberated—like me, in my loose skirts and slacks and my hair swinging free of the veil—the risks of rebelling are so high that we boil inside, but obey. We cling to the fading hope that someday we'll be released from this prison, not really believing that we can be the agents of our own freedom. Controlled by the fear generations of male dominance have instilled in us, a fear reinforced by our mothers, our only option seems to be to live carefully within the rules, regulations, and beliefs of the men who govern us. We absorb from birth that breaking the code is very, very dangerous. And yet, there are a few rare women who risk their lives to try. The whispers they hear are not from the desert, but from the winds of change.

ONE

*T*he cluttered break room in the back of N&D's Unisex Salon was not much to look at. Twenty years' worth of scuff marks marred the once-white walls and the tile floor whose warm earth beige once had shone, but which were now a dull yellow-gray. The scruffy brown couch to the right of the door looked like a battered old man, pockmarked by time. But Dalia, my best friend, and I knew the room's true value; to us it was a haven, a sanctuary, the only place where we had the privacy and freedom to share our secrets, hopes, dreams, fears, and disappointments.

That couch was the same one we'd sat on at the age of thirteen when we pledged that nothing and no one would ever destroy our friendship. We were like sisters, born a couple of months apart in 1970. Living as close neighbors in the Jebel Hussein district of Amman, we met at a neighborhood park when we were three and, almost instantly, were inseparable. We each had four brothers and very strict parents. And, despite the fact that we were from different religions—her family was strict Muslim, while mine was Catholic—we faced similar obstacles growing up that only strengthened the sisterly bond between us.

Though Jordan is a nation of rich and poor—the rich living in million-dollar villas and the poor in refugee camps—our families were part of the comfortable middle class that lived in houses handed down through their families for generations, and fathers who worked at respectable jobs; mine had his own contracting business, Dalia's was an accountant for a large insurance company. But we were not of the class that skimmed the cream of opportunities for women—the elite who automatically sent their daughters abroad to universities to live and study. Our parents never showed a hint of ambition for us, beyond marriage. By the time we entered our teenage years, we'd decided that we could forge the best future for ourselves by finding a way to stay together. At fifteen, we discovered that Jordanian women were allowed to own and operate beauty parlors, one of the few careers open to them. Higher dreams didn't seem possible. And Dalia and I believed that having our own business would guarantee that we could remain together. So, armed with a plan, we started taking the necessary steps to set up our business.

Our first move was to assure our parents that we were not college material. We easily maintained "C" averages, convincing them that this was the best we could do. In a country where a man's education carries more weight than a woman's, our lackluster performance did not worry either set of parents. Next, we suggested that we enroll in beauty school and, given our bleak college prospects, our families did not object—in fact they encouraged us to go. So, at eighteen, Dalia and I learned our trade. And, after finishing school and working at several places, we were able to complete our final step. Although we didn't see it at the time, we were already using one of the few powers Jordanian women have: to bend their intelligence and imagination to plotting and planning to outwit men to get what they wanted. We would become masters. It didn't occur to us that the effort we spent on conspiring and manipulation might have been turning us into doctors or software designers. Achievement was in tricking the men who controlled our lives; it was survival in an unequal world, as we saw it.

"You know, I think if we complain a bit longer about working at this salon, our fathers will agree to let us open our own place, if only to shut us up. My father seems ready to agree, how about yours?" Dalia asked me one day, her eyes betraying a hint of conspiratorial glee.

"Mine's getting tired of the complaints. But we'd better be careful; they could decide that we should stop working and stay home. I keep telling them that we love the work, we just hate the working conditions." I laughed.

"Me, too, and I think our fathers will go for it. Look at it from their point of view, they'll have an easier time keeping an eye on us this way." Until we were safely married and under the thumb of our husbands, we'd be watched every day, every hour, by our fathers and brothers.

ॐ

In the end, we persuaded our parents to invest a small fortune in our salon. Our idea was to renovate a portion of a two-story building owned by my father. No one had used the old, stonefront structure, which was close to both of our homes, for ten years; previously it had served as a warehouse for my father's contracting business. Neglected, covered with graffiti, and boarded up, it was destined for the wrecking ball until our plan salvaged it. In return for the use of the ground floor and as payment for the construction work my father and brothers did, we'd pay a monthly rent. To save some *masaree* (money), the break room was the only part of the salon we didn't modernize; it stayed as dingy as it was. But, behind its closed door, it was ours.

We were going to be daring and serve a need no other salon in Amman seemed to be serving: both men and women. As long as we were well watched and chaperoned, there was no prohibition against it. We held the grand opening of N&D's Unisex Salon in May 1990. The stone facade had been removed and a glass front put in its place. To us, the interior had been transformed into a mini-palace, with a high, vaulted ceiling. A large crystal chandelier was hung and the walls were mirrored, giving the illusion that the room was double its actual size. The mirrors reflected the chandelier's incandescent bulbs, bringing light to every corner of the shop. A high marble counter ingeniously hid our desk and separated the reception area from our workstations, each equipped with all the top styling tools. To us, this salon was more than just a dream come true, it made us feel invincible and powerful. Our modest little enterprise had turned us into professionals, entrepreneurs—we'd created our own niche. Though we had to some extent designed our own cage, a better one than what would have been created for us certainly, we were not outside of our families' ever-watchful eye. Dalia's brother Mohammed, assigned as our official watchdog, walked her to work every morning from the day we opened and kept a sharp eye on us through closing time. But nonetheless, we were convinced there was nothing we couldn't accomplish as long as we stuck together.

After the opening, we rather quickly managed to develop a healthy clientele and were good at turning our referrals into regulars. Our great haircuts, we decided, were the secret to our success, along with the friendly atmosphere and our quality customer service. The competing salons credited our shop's popularity to the fact that it was one of Amman's few salons owned and operated by women that catered to a mixed clientele. I've often wondered, if I had known that the decision to open the door to male customers would bring us such heartbreak down the road, would we have done it? I think, yes, we would have.

So, at twenty-five, we were still best friends. We'd kept the promise we'd made to each other years before, always stronger together than apart.

TWO

*L*ife in Dalia's home was basically like life in all Muslim homes in Amman, regardless of class, money, or neighborhood. She wasn't permitted to eat at the same table with, or at the same time as, the men in her household. She was to cook the meal and quietly serve it to them. Only when they had finished and left the room were she and her mother allowed to eat the leftovers. She was not allowed to leave her house unless she was accompanied by one of the men in her family. As if our neighborhood wasn't restrictive enough—houses have been in the same families for so long that they have achieved landmark status. It was possible to hail a cab from anywhere in Amman and reach your destination in Jebel Hussein by giving no more than a family name to the driver. Some people might appreciate this kind of closeness and familiarity, but to Dalia and me it was intrusive and, at times, suffocating.

Weeks into our first year of business it became clear that our designated chaperone, Mohammed, hated the early schedule; because he was always late we began to lose clients. It took us months of begging and pleading before our fathers finally allowed us to walk to the salon unaccompanied every morning. Now, Dalia would leave no later than eight to pick me up for work.

One morning, in March 1995, Dalia arrived ten minutes late and found me waiting on the terrace.

"Hey, *ya hilweh* [our joking slang for pretty or beautiful], are you ready to go or should I come up?" she shouted as she positioned herself beneath our balcony and gestured toward the stairs.

"I'm coming right down, *ya gazallae*," I yelled. *Ya gazallae* is slang for especially attractive women; it means with the melting eyes of a baby deer, like Bambi. Dalia definitely fit into that category. She had waist-length, thick, wavy tresses, perfect light olive skin, and full lips. Most of all, she had these mesmerizing dark brown eyes. Nature had put her only roundness in the proper places. I, on the other hand, was a bit shorter than she, with long black hair. My skin is smooth but my complexion is darker, and alas I always felt cursed with a pear-shaped body. An extra twenty or so pounds found their way to my hips when I was eighteen and refused to fade away.

I knew from the time we were young that I could never be as attractive as she was, but Dalia was more than just physically gorgeous. She had a way about her that would make anyone and everyone feel comfortable and beautiful around her. It was as if she were the only one who couldn't see that her looks far surpassed ours. What completed Dalia's rare package was that the beauty was backed by intelligence and strength.

I bounded off the last stair, wound my arm around Dalia's, and announced, "Let's go." We walked arm-in-arm through the winding streets of our neighborhood of Jebel Hussein until we reached the salon. We knew every block and building in our close community, knew the pride most families took in their descending from the original nomadic tribes that settled there. With the lack of green plants and flowers, the area still had the spirit and pervasive dun color of the old clusters of goat-hair tents in the desert.

At the salon, we usually worked side by side, handling one client after the next, from 8:30 until 2:30, with a couple of hours off for lunch and coffee. It was a good existence, but it lacked the exhilaration we thought we'd find when we opened the salon.

That afternoon, I walked the last customer to the exit, leaned my back against the door, slowly sliding to the floor, and exhaled loudly.

"Finally! Finished. I'm so tired. I didn't get much sleep last night," I said as I sat on the floor with my legs stretched in front of me.

Dalia turned toward me with a playfully wicked grin. "Why not? What were you doing?"

"Nothing, I just couldn't sleep. I had too much on my mind."

"Like what?"

"I don't know. Maybe I just need a vacation or something, I think I'm bored. I'm going to try to get some rest in the back."

Dalia was careful not to push me.

It took all my strength to stand and drag myself across the room. I paused briefly when I reached Dalia to exhale exaggeratedly, and then continued into the break room. I sat on the arm of the couch and dumped myself onto its cushions. Memories that rose from sleepless nights filled my brain. For the past week or so I'd been restless and preoccupied. I didn't know why, but I was now analyzing every aspect of my life and craving change. Every morning as the cold *Rabeey* winds beckoned me to get up, I secretly hoped they'd brought something different or new with them.

Dalia came into the break room a few minutes later and found me lying on the couch staring at the ceiling. She slid a cigarette out of her pack and tossed it to me. "Here, maybe this will help." In my mood, it only reinforced how pathetically shrunken our lives were that a taboo cigarette seemed like a great adventure. But I took it.

"Are you sure we won't get caught?" I asked as I lit the cigarette.

"Relax. I locked the doors. And, anyway, Mohammed took his friend Raed to the market. They should be gone for at least an hour. I asked them to pick up some fresh-squeezed carrot juice. I thought that would delay them."

She strolled over to the couch and sat beside me, her face animated.

"Remember when we first did this?" she asked, looking at the cigarette. She was fighting the urge to laugh at the thought of my red face and wide, tear-filled eyes.

"I should have known then what a bad influence you would be," I replied.

"You were so scared."

"I was *not!* I was choking!"

"Everyone chokes their first time," Dalia said before bursting into uncontrollable laughter.

"Well, you could have warned me," I mumbled.

"Don't tell me you're still holding a grudge? Anyway, I did warn you in my own way," she managed to say between bursts of laughter.

"Oh, sure," I said, in a mocking voice.

Dalia left to tidy up our workstations, and when she returned a few minutes later, our petty chatting suddenly turned electric.

"Did you see that guy who was in here earlier?" she asked as she sat down next to me on the couch, close enough for a whisper.

What? In all the years I'd known her, she'd never mentioned a specific man, unless she was criticizing him. She'd always viewed men as the enemy and marriage as the ultimate defeat, since she knew she'd be forced to forfeit her few liberties, such as the salon, if she married.

"Which one?" I asked, snapping my head to face her.

"The one in the army uniform, the gorgeous one!"

The gorgeous one! "I can't believe this. You've never called a man gorgeous before."

"I know, I know, but did you see him?" she asked impatiently, eyes lit by a strange new excitement.

Of course I'd seen him. The fact that he was the only client who'd come in wearing an army uniform made him easier to remember. "I'm not blind."

"That's the third time he's been here in the past two weeks."

"What does he want? Who is he?"

"Each time he comes in, he says that he wants a haircut and tells me to take a little off the ends. Then he spends the whole time talking to me. But I don't mind. Just looking at him feels good."

Tall, quite a bit taller than Dalia, I remembered, racking my brain to recall exactly what he looked like, this man who'd suddenly entered our intimate space, perhaps to cause trouble for my best friend. What if her brother, Mohammed, had noticed him? Mohammed was not only our watchdog, but he was our fathers' hired, loyal informant. What if he reported it to her father—Dalia flirting with a strange man?

"Dalia, you can't let anyone else hear you say that," I said. Broad shoulders, thick, short, dark brown hair, black eyes—an image was coming.

"I know, but I can say it to you. Anyway, all I'm doing is looking and talking right now. But, I think he likes me. I mean, come on, he's been in for three haircuts in two weeks. Plus I've caught him staring at me," she said happily.

His eyes were dark and penetrating with thick brows and long, thick lashes.

"Do you like him? Do you think you could like him romantically? And *why* haven't you told me about this sooner? I'm supposed to be your best friend."

Small, straight nose, full lips, square jawline, thin mustache. He'd look better without the mustache, but they seemed to be an Arab man's fashion statement. I had my picture of him.

"Relax, I'll tell you everything," she said.

"Come on, I want all the details." We may have been twenty-five, but we were so inexperienced that we were chatting like a pair of adolescents over a first crush. But for me, this was more than girlish gossip. It felt urgent, like a detective's interrogation. Dalia was being driven by some inner fire that shone through her eyes.

"Normie, calm down. There's not much to report. His name is Michael, he's thirty-two and a major in the Royal Guard. He has three sisters and two brothers. He's the oldest in his family. He's intelligent, handsome, charming, polite, unlike the men in our families. She lowered her voice. "And he's Catholic."

You have to be a Jordanian woman to grasp what a shock, a frightening explosive shock, those words were. My response just rushed out. *"Bism il lah* [Oh my God, in the name of God], Dalia! You have to forget about him, now! Nothing but trouble can come from this." Both Jordanian society and law strictly forbade relationships between people of different religions. But what chilled me as I heard this were all the stories I'd heard about the tragic endings of these relationships. They seldom reached the papers. You heard about them as gossip, in the neighborhood, in the salon—what award-winning gossip journalists some of our friends and customers would have made. Women had died or been sent to prison for life because their families suspected them of having a secret romantic relationship while they were single, let alone a relationship with someone of a different religion.

But it was far more real to us than gossip. We'd lost a seventeen-year-old client to an honor killing. How could Dalia forget? This girl had been molested by a close male relative—she'd *told* us! And she'd been killed—we had to assume by the men in her family—to keep it quiet.

"All we're doing is talking. What harm can come from that? I admit it. I'm attracted to him, and I think he's attracted to me, but we've just talked." She was blinded, oblivious. "Anyway, you know how I feel about religion. We're all born into a religion, but it's something we have no control over. If I was born Catholic, then I'd be Catholic. But I was born Muslim and so I'm Muslim. Look at us, you're Catholic. But that has nothing to do with loving you—or anyone—more or less."

Dalia had always made her views about religion clear, but this was different. I'd never heard her defend a man, and the passion in her voice and the look in her eyes told me more than any words. She was in love; she just didn't know it yet.

For all her incredible strength, she seemed as vulnerable as Bambi, and I suddenly felt tender. "Oh, *gazallae,* you know I feel the same way you do about religion, but our families don't see it the way we do. The whole country is prejudiced against this kind of thing. I love you too much to see you get hurt, especially over someone you hardly even know."

"I know, Norma. I understand that you're worried, but I'm not going to get hurt. While I've only talked to him three times, there's something about him . . . I don't know what it is. I can't explain it. When I talk to him, I feel as if nothing else exists or matters. I know it sounds stupid, but I feel as if I've known him all my life," she said ecstatically.

"Well, it sounds as if you more than just like him."

"I don't know. I've never felt this way before. It's different, it's exciting and scary and wonderful, all at the same time. I can't explain it."

"So I take it you want to continue to talk to this man?" I asked, knowing I was falling short of being as wise as I wanted to be.

"*Yes!* Definitely. I know I shouldn't, but it's not something I can control. Who knows, maybe it's my destiny."

"Destiny, did you say your *destiny?* But you don't believe in destiny. Anyway, how do you plan to keep talking to him? Don't you think Mohammed will get suspicious if he keeps coming in for haircuts? I mean, after two more appointments, he'll be bald. What's he going to use as an excuse after that?"

"I'll worry about my brother. Right now, I need you to help me find a way to see him again, please. Together I'm sure we can come up with something."

"Dalia, is it that important to you? Do you realize the risk you'll be taking? Do you think he's worth the risk?" This was her chance to hear me, to open her eyes. Please, Dalia, please.

"I think so. *Yes.*" She said it with a fervor that frightened me.

"Okay, then. I'm sure I'll regret this, but you know I'll help you. We have to be careful. If we're caught, we'll both be in serious trouble." I made one last try. "Why would you want to pursue this when you won't be allowed to marry him?"

"I know I won't, but I'm not thinking about that right now. I just feel as if I have to see him and talk to him again, even if he just becomes my secret friend and nothing more."

"Okay." I hugged her shoulder and got up from the couch. "We can talk about this again tomorrow. Right now you'd better go unlock the doors while I straighten up and clean out the ashtrays. We don't want Mohammed and Raed to find the place looking like this. They'll be here soon."

"Thanks, thanks so much." Dalia was almost bouncing as she went to unlock the doors.

As I tidied up the break room, I wondered if I was doing the right thing by helping Dalia enter into such a relationship. I tried to convince myself that Dalia was right—that we two could do anything as long as we did it together.

We had learned girls' rules together. Now, at twenty-five, for the first time in our lives, we were specifically thinking of challenging them. When we were little, neither society nor our families distinguished between the boys and girls. It didn't seem to matter where, how, or with whom we played. But as time went on, our list of rules steadily grew, until by the age of ten, we were no longer allowed to associate with boys not related to us. We never questioned the reasons for this change, since we were at an age when we preferred to play with girls anyway. Looking back, it's clear that the foundation of our future was being built then, but in a way that felt gradual, incontestable, and unavoidable.

Our mothers, like all mothers of daughters, did their job by training us to live in an unsympathetic, protected, male-dominated world. I'm certain no woman raised in Jordan has escaped her childhood and young adulthood without hearing things like: "A woman's honor, once ruined, can never be repaired," or "Better to lose your life than lose your reputation." They told us about the woman who chose to kill herself and die honorably rather than allow a potential rapist to assault her, and of the woman who didn't preserve her honor and was raped only to be murdered by her own family who were protecting their "good" name.

Our parents wove into everyday life the idea that all men are superior to women. We were not beaten into a state of slavery with whips and chains, but rather persuaded into it by the words and teachings of centuries-old traditions. It was not our faith in those words that continued to bind us but our fear of the consequences if we ever went against them. This was the first time that either of us had ever thought of challenging these conventions.

When we'd finished cleaning up and had hidden our cigarettes, we unbolted the doors and sat at my station to wait for Dalia's brother and his friend. Fifteen minutes later we heard a pickup pull up in front of the salon and Mohammed got out, laughing and talking loudly. He rushed in and dropped off our carrot juice and falafel sandwiches. To our surprise he only stayed long enough to find out when he should come to take us home and lock up. Then, he made a quick phone call to confirm that his friend still wanted to go to Auto World. This was a thrilling day for him; his friend had managed to hunt down the tire rims he'd been searching for since he'd bought the pickup. After he'd hung up, he dashed out of the salon, yelling, "Call me on my cell phone if you need anything," and disappeared into the gloomy afternoon.

Mohammed loved his pickup. He'd bought it the previous October and saw it as far more than a means of transportation. It was his hobby, his baby, his full-time job. Although he'd bought it loaded with all the possible options, he was ceaselessly improving it.

For Dalia and me, Mohammed's preoccupation with the pickup was the answer to our prayers. It gave us hours of private time together.

For years the only Mohammed-free moments we'd had were during lunch. With him reporting home, not much had happened during the four and a half years we'd operated the salon that our fathers didn't know about. While Dalia and I didn't appreciate having a spy in our midst, we had no control over it. If we complained, it would only make our families suspect that we had something to hide. It would go against everything we'd been taught.

Like most Jordanian women, Dalia and I did not have the right to argue with the men in our families. Even if we were right, the simple fact that we were female made us wrong in the eyes of society. We had no right to challenge the principle. It was a universal Arabic creed, one that cut across religion and class.

THREE

Dalia had been agitated all morning. Now, as I was wrapping up a perm on my five o'clock appointment a few days after the Michael revelation, she sat at the front counter flipping through a magazine. She had forty minutes free before her next client and although she was reading about new hairstyle trends and fashions, she was obviously preoccupied with thoughts of Michael. Now she was rummaging through the piles of papers and notebooks we'd accumulated over the years, restlessly trying to keep herself busy.

"You know, we really should clean some of this out," she said as she pulled out a notebook with the word "Scorebook" written in black across the cover. "I think we can stop keeping score—it's pretty obvious that I've won, don't you think?" she said, holding the notebook up for me to see. This was a cryptic inside joke between us that went over the head of Lucy, the young girl nervously waiting to see the result of her perm.

Dalia opened it to the first page. July 26, 1990, was written in bold red letters. She leaned back in her chair and closed her eyes. It had begun innocently enough, with a chat about one of Dalia's regular clients who'd been in that morning. Um Suhal was pregnant with her second child. During her appointment Dalia asked her whether she was hoping to have a boy or girl, and her reply—a boy—later led to one of her diatribes.

"Norma, you know what's really weird?" she asked.

"What?" The look in her eyes told me that I was in for a long, drawn-out lecture on the state of life in Jordan and the plight of Jordanian women, in particular.

"Why is it that every time you ask a pregnant woman if she wants boy or a girl, she always says a boy?"

"Oh, come on, the women who say that probably only do so to make their husbands happy. You know all men want a son."

"I think there has to be more to it than that," she announced. And so we'd started keeping score in our Scorebook.

In the years we'd been keeping the scorebook, we'd asked 193 women. Only 15 of them said they wanted girls, the remaining 178 wanted boys. This was all the evidence Dalia needed. As the numbers increased in her favor over the years, so did her passion for reform. She envisioned a New World for women, a place where we would share equal rights with men. A place where we'd have the right to make our own choices and decisions about all the issues that influenced our lives—careers, marriage, and family. Where a pregnant woman would want to have a girl.

Waving the Scorebook at me, she was trying to bait me to state her theory, as she had so many times in the past.

I knew she wouldn't let up until I said it.

"I wouldn't want any daughter of mine to grow up like this—to be a man's slave. And I wouldn't want her to grow up in a place where she's considered a second-class citizen," I said, hoping to end the discussion.

"See, that's it, Norma, that's my point exactly. I think that's the real reason every woman has said she wants a boy. They don't think they can fight it, so let's hope it's a boy."

A flash of victory showed on her face. But this was only the beginning of her theory. She was turning our little salon into a revolutionary platform.

"I believe that a lot of women think like us. And, if that's true, sooner or later things will have to change," she proclaimed, cueing me to play devil's advocate.

"Why do you assume that? There's nothing they can do to change things, just like there's nothing we can do."

"You're wrong. Our mothers' generation lived like this because they believed in the Arab way of life, not because they were afraid to take a stand. We live like this because we're afraid, not because we believe in it. So sooner or later things will have to change."

"Dalia, I think you need to face reality. For all the cell phones and computers and even some women doctors and activists— what's changed for us? People in this country have had these customs and beliefs for centuries, and it'll take centuries to change their way of thinking," I protested.

"I don't think so. True, they've had these beliefs for centuries. But, as you said yourself, our generation of women doesn't believe, it *fears*. Fear can be overcome. Think about it—when someone fears something, there's a chance she may one day find the courage she needs to force a change. But if she *believes* in the status quo, she has no need to change it. If our generation doesn't change things, then maybe the next one will or the one after that, but eventually the fear will be overcome and changes will be made. Change always follows, you'll see."

∂°℃

I, and many of Dalia's other friends, believed the same thing, treasured the same dreams. But we were silent dreamers. Dalia would be the first to protest in the streets, while the rest of us stood by. We lacked the courage, or the passion, to take it that far. But despite her leadership, she made other women feel equal to her, pulling us along to higher levels of courage. She was always highlighting the positives about you, making it impossible to feel inadequate in her presence. She was a force of nature, driven by an inner power I can only describe as a gift. But I can understand how Jordanian men would find a woman like Dalia as menacing as an attacking army.

To Middle Eastern men, Dalia's beliefs made her an enemy, a *sharmuta*, and they would have only one way to deal with her. They would silence her before she had the chance to influence others with her scandalous views. The long-established way to abolish *sharmutas* was execution. There would be no questions, no judge, no jury, and no chance for a defense. Her death wouldn't warrant an investigation or cause the filing of any criminal charges. Her death would be considered justifiable since she was a threat to the Jordanian quality of life and to the customs, morals, and values Jordanian society had upheld for thousands of years.

I'd feared for my friend's life for years, while I envied her spirit. How many times had I warned her, "You're blessed with an angel's face but cursed with a devil's tongue." Not because anything she said was wrong, but because everything she said was critical of ancient laws. Desert laws.

For buried deep within the history of Jordan was a secret way of life, with its source in the nomadic Bedouins, the desert dwellers. Though they make up less than one percent of the Jordanian population, they and their views dominate the country. Some have opted for city life and many have settled down to cultivate crops rather than drive their animals across the desert in search of food. However, approximately forty thousand Bedouin choose to continue living according to the old ways. They camp for a few months at a time in one spot and graze their animals. Their black goat-hair tents (known as *beit ash shair*) are all over the east and south of Jordan. Such tents are usually separated—a harem for the women and a section for men, which is where modern segregation in our homes, mosques, and public places comes from.

Most men of the desert continue to wear the traditional long flowing robes, along with a dagger, which symbolizes a man's dignity. Women tend to dress in layers upon layers of more colorful garb, making sure they are completely covered. Unlike some Muslim women, they rarely veil their faces, opting for intricate patterns of facial tattoos instead. Similar to their modern counterparts, their heads and hair must always be veiled when in the presence of men, and although female infanticide and female circumcision are extremely rare among Jordan's urban citizens, it's not unheard of among the desert dwellers. This nomadic, ancient lifestyle gave birth to the traditional and secretive way of life that still dominates most of the Arab world and pervades our lives in Amman. It is a way of life so important to, and idealized by, Arab men that they will not hesitate to sacrifice women in an attempt to preserve it.

FOUR

*I*t had been a little over two weeks since Dalia or I had seen or heard from Michael, and we searched for excuses for why he hadn't come in. He didn't love her . . . or maybe he loved her so much he was protecting her from risk. He'd been in a terrible accident and was maimed, perhaps killed. Dalia began each day hoping he would appear or at least call, but as the hours crept by, worry would cloud her face. By closing time, she looked as if she were going to a wake. She tried to keep disappointment and bitterness away as the excitement she'd felt began to turn into a growing fear that she might never see him again.

For the first three or four days after his last haircut, our conversations had been dominated by Michael. We conjured up countless scenarios for how Dalia could see him again, without anyone who knew her ever seeing her with him; we came up with plans. We remembered the risks involved, but, for some reason, believed we would not be found out.

Sometimes Dalia tried to pretend she didn't care whether she saw him again. He was only a client, like any other. But she was not convincing; her anguish showed more each day.

As the third week was drawing to a close, Dalia was dragging herself around the salon silently cleaning up as I prepared for the final client of the day. The client was a referral named Jehan, who had called in the morning and begged me to fit her into today's schedule. I knew from the way Dalia felt that she would refuse to take her, but she sounded so desperate that I didn't have the heart to turn her away. I glanced at my watch and saw that I still had about ten minutes before Jehan was due to arrive. I wanted to talk to Dalia about the way she was feeling but had no idea how to begin. Neither of us had any experience with love, so I just decided to avoid the whole subject. When she was ready to talk, she would. But she was descending into deeper depression. Minutes stretched into hours as I watched Dalia, and waited for Jehan, feeling frozen in time. I'd try to envision our future and the vision of more of the past frightened me. For the first time in my life I wondered if this salon was our destiny—if we were destined to remain single all of our lives. The thought of being married to an Arab man turned my stomach, as it did Dalia's, but this first realization that I might end up totally alone disturbed me. How would I feel if I found myself attracted to a Muslim man? I wondered, as the gravity of Dalia's dilemma began to weigh heavily on my mind. How would my parents and brothers react to something like that? The killing and imprisonment of women who broke the rules wasn't just Islamic; it crossed religious lines. Now that the informal affection of childhood had been replaced with rigid control over me, I could picture my brothers battling with my father over who would cast the first stone.

ॐ∞ॐ

If you learn nothing else growing up in Jordan, you learn two things very early: the first, that Muslims and Christians must never intermarry, and the second, which was just as important, that you must never lose composure in public regardless of how serious your personal problems were. I suspect that no other nationality ever believed so vehemently in that old aphorism "Never air your dirty laundry in public." For example, Christians and Muslims were friendly and hospitable toward one another in public, but they would never, ever let their children marry.

The world would never see this. My brothers had worked very hard over the years to maintain the "honorable family image" my parents insisted we portray. If you met my brothers in public, you'd find four well-educated, professional, refined young gentlemen. Ranging from twenty-three to thirty-two, from average-looking to handsome, they appear to be modern young Arab men. But this is a facade that demonstrates none of the dynamic that has gone on behind the closed doors of our home.

There my brothers' true natures were revealed. While my brothers' friends might have difficulty picturing them reacting with violence if they found I was romantically interested in a man, it was easy for me to imagine. My brothers' fierce natures would not surprise any Arab woman who knew from birth that what women call brutal, men define as necessary. These were the secrets hidden from the street. All Arab men are taught that it is their responsibility to discipline the women in their lives, and that the best way to do so is through corporal punishment. My brothers were no exception. It was not uncommon to hear of women being physically abused not only by their husbands or fathers, but also by their sons and brothers, for simple reasons—preparing the wrong food for dinner, or taking too long with the laundry. Though my father and brothers were lenient about such trivial things, I didn't doubt for a second that they would react violently over more serious matters, such as relationships.

I dreaded the look of dismay and disdain I knew would come over my mother's round and lovely face if I ever did something to truly anger them. She was nearing fifty-four and was short and pleasantly stocky. She had creamy white skin, high pink color in her cheeks, and black eyes that twinkled like bright stars. Sometimes when I looked into her eyes, I sensed that the gleam reflected the tears hidden behind her cheerful spirit. There were days I would catch her sitting alone, when she thought no one could see her, with a distant look in her eyes, as if picturing herself in another life. I sensed I was glimpsing ghosts of lost opportunities tucked away in her heart. But she forced herself to live this illusion, rationalizing that if she pretended to be satisfied long enough she would one day wake up content.

My father, though more threatening in size, would probably be the least physically explosive of all my family members. In contrast to his formidable appearance, he was a very sedate man who, even if profoundly upset, would never visibly show it. If I ever formed a romantic relationship with a Muslim man, he might not lift the fist or knife, but he would be the driving force behind my brothers' violent acts.

I was brought out of these thoughts by the front door closing. Standing nervously in front of the door was a tall, slim young woman with an impressive mane of sable hair pulled into a thick, silky ponytail that hung to her hips. Dalia was nowhere to be seen. She must have gone to the break room to rest, I assumed, as I stepped toward the front counter to welcome Jehan. A moment later the door opened again and in walked Michael, not maimed or killed, but—it suddenly occurred to me—perhaps married. Since he was with Jehan, he could only be her husband or a relative; given the hour, it was more than likely that he was her husband. My mind started racing—Why hadn't he told Dalia? How *could* he bring his wife in here? What if he wasn't attracted to Dalia at all? Didn't he realize that Dalia was attracted to him? I knew that Michael and Dalia would never be able to marry, not in Jordan anyway, but there had seemed to be some chemistry between them. I prayed it was not just Dalia's fantasy. Finding out that Michael was married would send her into an even deeper funk.

Instinctively, I felt I had to protect my friend and find out what was going on before alerting her that Michael was back. At the counter, I tried not to betray my emotions.

"Hi, can I help you?"

"I'm Jehan. I have an appointment with Norma," she said, confident and friendly.

"I'm Norma, it's nice to meet you. Are you two together?" I asked, looking directly at Michael.

"Yes, we are," he said swiftly, leaving me searching for something to say. "Come with me," I finally muttered. Jehan followed me to my station while Michael remained in the reception area. An awful thought ran through my mind: What if he hadn't told her he'd been here before? I had to tread very carefully. But for Dalia's sake, I also had to get some answers.

As Jehan was seated, I hoped that she was like most of my clients, who used the stylist's chair as a psychiatrist's couch, chatting and spilling the details of their personal lives until they stood up to leave.

"What would you like done?" I asked.

"Well, he managed to convince me that I'd look better with shoulder-length hair, so here I am," she said with a spectacular smile.

"He who?" I asked, trying to pry a whisper of useful data from her.

33

"Michael, of course. He's been recommending this place to me for weeks. He said that this is the best salon in Amman, and that Dalia is great."

"Oh . . . well I'm glad to hear that. You must be very close if you trust his advice about your hair," I asked, still fishing.

"Oh, yes, we're very close. He's great and very sweet, unlike most men, if you know what I mean. And he's so smart. His is the only opinion I value, not just about my hair, but in every aspect of my life."

I still didn't know if they were married, so I determined to keep quiet and hoped that she would lead the conversation where I needed it to go. I glanced over at Michael sitting in the reception area. He'd picked a seat where he could view the entire salon. He held a magazine, partly hiding his face, but I could see he was spending much more time looking around than reading it. He was wriggling, appeared anxious and uncomfortable, which mystified me more. If Jehan was his wife and he was worried about bumping into Dalia, why bring her here?

I tried a gentle probe to get Jehan to open up. "Where do you usually get your hair done?"

"I normally go to Mary's in the second circle. Have you heard of it?"

"Yes. It's across the street from Abu Ali's Bakery, right? Do you live near Mary's?"

"Actually, we live an equal distance between here and there. We live in Abdoun, next to the fourth circle."

"I know where that is," I said, disheartened at the "we." There was no mistaking that when she said "we," she meant she and Michael. I didn't want to show my disappointment, but I knew I had the answer I was looking for. She clearly lived with Michael.

She must be his wife. All I wanted to do was finish her hair and get them both out of the salon before Dalia saw them.

I thought of Dalia, who was just a wall away in the break room. How was I supposed to tell her that he was here? That he was married? That Jehan was a sweet, attractive, pleasant girl, someone we might have been friends with under different circumstances, would upset her even more. As I subdued my desire to mangle Jehan's mane (it wasn't her fault, after all), I wished I could get my hands on what little was left of Michael's hair.

I heard Mohammed's pickup thundering up the street just as I steered Jehan to the front of the salon. "Well, Michael, what do you think?" she asked as she twirled her head and ran her fingers through her hair.

"It looks great," he replied, then stopped cold as he saw Dalia stroll up to the front counter. Jehan turned to see what he was staring at. Dalia looked confused, but before I could speak, Mohammed burst through the front door.

He found the four of us standing motionless and staring silently at one another. The tension was so sharp and the room so silent that all I could hear was the sound of my heart beating. Mohammed sliced through the stillness. "Are you ready to close up?" Michael and Jehan took that as their cue to escape. As they walked out, Dalia looked at me with a mixture of anguish, ecstasy, and sheer bewilderment. I dreaded our lunch tomorrow, the first time we'd have to talk.

FIVE

Two weeks later, we still hadn't found a moment to be alone. So I set out for Dalia's at 5:30 one morning, praying that we would find some time to talk before heading to the salon. I had to tell Dalia that I thought Michael was married. To our dismay, Mohammed's social calendar had been blank for the last three weeks, so he'd spent all of his time with us, taking up residence in our break room.

My father and brothers had left the night before to visit my grandfather, my mother's father, who lived in the farmhouse near Irbid. So, that morning I was free from my regular chores. I raced to Dalia's house, planning to get there after her morning prayers but before she had to begin her chores.

I arrived at the house and stood for a moment, as I caught my breath before knocking. Dalia's mother appeared at the door with a pail of grimy water. Obviously not expecting anyone to be standing there, she jumped back, startled, when she saw me.

"*Bism il lah* [oh my God]," she exclaimed. "*Sabah al-khair* [good morning]. What are you doing here so early?"

"I'm sorry, I didn't mean to startle you. *Sabah al-noor*, Um Suhal, I came to see Dalia."

"Of course you did. Where's my mind? Go on in, if she's not in the kitchen she should be in her room."

"Thank you, Um Suhal. But can I help with that first?"

"No, no, you go on in."

For as long as I could remember Dalia's mom had been called Um Suhal, which means "mother of Suhal." With the birth of a woman's first son she loses her own identity. From the day of her son's birth, she is referred to as "mother of———." Fathers are renamed similarly, but with a twist. Men are valued both before and after their child's arrival. They are recognized for having created such a valuable child—a son—and thus are given the name "Abu———." But, unlike his wife, a father also continues to use his real name.

Um Suhal, whose real name was Rania, was a very fragile-looking creature, the opposite of my more stocky mother. She was tall and slender, with a yellowish-white complexion that must have been like fresh rose petals once, but had now lost its youthful luster. Her small, emerald green eyes were also marked by time. Whatever fires they had contained had burned out years ago, leaving them gloomy and dim. She was one of a small cluster of Arabs who still show signs of their ancient Greco-Roman genes, a group of women considered scarce and highly sought after by Arab men. Women with fair skin, light hair, and eyes that were neither black nor brown were deemed more than just attractive, they were believed to produce the most handsome offspring. Looking at Dalia and her four brothers, you'd believe the theory clearly held a lot of truth.

I found Dalia in her room, sitting on her bed, reading the last few pages of Taher al Edwar's *The Fact of Time.*

"*Sabah al-khair, ya gazallae.* What are you reading?" I announced as I walked into her room.

"Oh my God. How did you manage to escape so early this morning?" she asked as she stood up to embrace me.

"I got lucky, my father and brothers went to check on *Gidi* [my grandfather], and I ran over here so we could finally talk."

"I'm so glad you did, I feel as if I'm going to burst. First, let's make sure the coast is clear." She bolted out of the room.

I sat on her bed and looked around at her possessions, noting how many of them reflected our friendship. Some of the things dated back to our childhoods—the fossils we found at the age of seven while playing on my family's farm, or the candy dish that housed her collection of sea shells, bits of coral, and starfish that we discovered on the coast of Aqaba. Others were more recent, including the Samar Hadaddin canvas we'd bought at Riwak Al Balkaa Art Gallery in Fuheis a few weeks before and now hung above her headboard. The painting's mate hung in my room, as the artist, a woman, had quickly become our favorite.

While Dalia's furnishings, comforter, and curtains were clearly chosen by her mother, everything else reflected her.

She came back holding two small *fanageen* (small Turkish coffee cups) brimming with coffee.

"Pull out the folding table from behind the dresser," she said. After I positioned the little table near the bed, she set down the coffee and started rummaging through the bottom drawer of her dresser.

"Close and lock the door," she stated. Seconds later she pulled out a pack of Gauloise Blondes, matches, and a small, handmade earthenware ashtray. Then, before sitting on the bed, she grabbed the radio from her window ledge, switched it on, lowered the volume, and placed it on the floor behind the locked door so no one walking along the corridor could listen to our conversation.

"Now we can talk," she said as she handed me a cigarette. I placed the cigarette on the table next to my coffee and turned to her.

"You're not going to like what I have to say," I started.

"What do you mean?" She was steeling herself, composing herself.

"Well, I think Michael may be married." A wild range of emotions played across her face as she tried to stay poised.

"I don't think so. I mean he's not the kind of person who would hide something like that."

"You remember Jehan, the woman he brought to the salon? Well, they came together and left together and it was late in the day."

"That doesn't mean that she's his wife."

"No, but they live together, too."

"That still doesn't mean that she's his wife. Did she say she was his wife?"

"No, but she did say that she loves and respects him."

"Well, she can love and respect him if she's his relative."

"I know, but at that hour, Dalia, most single women aren't allowed out. You know that. We'd only be allowed to go to a relative's home at that time."

"I know, but still, she could be a married relative, a cousin, or . . . She lives with him? Are you sure?"

"Yes, I'm sure."

"Well then, she's probably one of his sisters. He has three, you know."

"I didn't remember that. I suppose she could have been his sister, but if she's not his sister, promise me that you won't talk to him again."

40

"I can't promise that. I mean, if she's his wife, then I won't want to talk to him again."

"Good."

"How can we find out who she is? Did he say anything that night? Did you talk to him?"

"I didn't get a chance to, I was working on Jehan's hair most of the time. If we want to find out who she is, we're going to have to talk to them again. Maybe we could call her and say that we're having a promotion at the salon and that she was randomly chosen from a list of new clients to receive a free facial or something. If she comes in again, we might be able to figure out how she and Michael are related."

"That just might work. Let's call her today."

"Okay," I said as I lit my cigarette.

A few minutes later, we were interrupted by a loud knock on the door, followed by her brother Rafiq's voice bellowing, "Dalia, where's the coffee?"

"*Hiene jia* [I'm coming]," she hollered as she gave me an exasperated look.

Rafiq, although the youngest of her four brothers, was one of the cruelest, most argumentative young men I've ever known. Although he was gorgeous, his temperament was reflected in his physical image, leaving him ugly, in my opinion.

"Let me help you make breakfast, that way you'll finish faster and we'll have more time to talk," I said.

"Okay, that sounds good."

Dalia hid the cigarettes and matches and sprayed air freshener, while I emptied the ashtray in the bathroom and flushed away the incriminating butts. I followed her to the kitchen, where, after preparing a gallon of mint tea and Turkish coffee, we began to cook breakfast. First the *eejay*—eggs, onions, flour, and spices, mixed together into a semi-runny batter and fried—and then the fried tomatoes. Then we arranged the *laban* (a cheese spread), *zayt* and *zayter* (an olive oil and spices bread dip), olives, *ka'ik* (biscuits), and Arabic bread on the table. Our job complete, we refilled our coffee cups and went out to the back patio. Um Suhal came into the kitchen as we were leaving and began taking out the tea and coffee cups. When Dalia's brothers and father came down, she would serve them before leaving the kitchen so they could eat. Dalia normally had to help her mother tidy the bedrooms and do the laundry as the men ate their food, but since I was there, she was excused.

We sat on wrought-iron chairs on Dalia's patio, a large, cement slab shaded by a prehistoric grapevine fastened to a metal canopy, and placed our coffee on the marble top of the wrought-iron table. The shade from the ancient grapevine was pleasant and the coffee good. We sat in silence for a while, taking pleasure in the morning calm. Since the back patio was near the kitchen, we didn't want to resume our conversation for fear that Dalia's father and brothers would hear us through the open window.

All of the men in Dalia's family were in the kitchen except for her brother Nasar, who was married and had moved out nine months before. Nasar was an older and, if possible, nastier version of Rafiq. He worked as an agricultural engineer at a government office. His wife, Diana, had a dental degree, but had never been allowed to work, either before her wedding or now. She wasn't allowed to leave the house without Nasar, even to take out the garbage. The one time she complained, he broke her nose and sent her back to her family, who told her that he was well within his rights and that she deserved what she got for trying to defy him.

Then they sent her back to beg his forgiveness. In the nine months of their marriage, she had left the apartment four times, once when he allowed her to accompany him to the *Abai'ala* (supermarket), once to go to her family's home, and twice to visit Dalia's home.

After Dalia's brother Suhal dropped us off in front of N&D's, and waited for us to unlock the door and go into the salon before he left, Dalia announced,

"Now we have to find that Jenah's or Jehan's number and set something up with her. Since you worked on her hair, you make the call."

"I knew you were going to make me call!" Then, with a dramatic sigh of resignation, she said, "Okay, I'll do it."

Six

The phone rang five times before someone answered. As it was ringing, I almost lost my nerve and hung up, but when I tried to return the receiver to its base, Dalia grabbed my arm and held it firmly in place.

Finally I heard a man's voice. I stiffened, and Dalia knew that someone had answered. I couldn't just hang up. I froze, unable to speak, until Dalia nudged me and my practiced script poured out, but so formally that it must have sounded like a recorded message.

"Hello, I'm calling from N&D's Salon. May I please speak to Jehan?" I asked, and held my breath.

"Dalia, is that you?" The voice sounded nervous.

"No, it's Norma. Is this Michael?" I asked before I realized what I was saying. Then I felt my panic starting to mount.

"Yes, it is. Norma, where's Dalia? How is she? Can I speak with her?" he asked in one breath, before I cut in, feeling my courage increasing.

"Why should I tell you how she is? Or where she is?" I said, astonished to hear the words coming out of my mouth. After all, I had never been so direct or frank with a man before.

"Norma, please, I'm begging you, put her on the phone. I

haven't been able to forget the look she gave me the last time I was at the salon. I can't sleep. I can't even work. I called in sick today, that's why I'm here. Don't worry, I'm alone. My mother went to the supermarket with my uncle. If Dalia's there, just let me hear her voice," Michael said. This was the sort of outpouring I could never, before then, have imagined coming from a man.

"What about your wife?" I asked, bracing for his reply.

"My what? I'm not married. Who said I was married?" he said, sounding genuinely shocked.

"Well, no one, but if you're not, then who is Jehan?"

"Jehan's my baby sister. You thought she was my wife?" he blurted out. He began laughing, though it was a relieved and lovely, rather than mocking, laugh.

"Well, what was I supposed to think? It was quite late when you came in and I assumed that your family, like mine, doesn't let your sisters out at that hour."

"Oh, that is so funny. She's *not* my wife, she's my little sister. Now, please, where's Dalia?"

"She's here next to me. We don't have any appointments for the next hour, so I can put her on."

"Please, please do," he urged.

I tried to hand Dalia the phone, but she pushed it away, her face turning beet red. I covered the mouthpiece and whispered, "What are you doing? It's Michael. He's home alone and wants to talk to you."

"I can't, Norma. I want to, but I can't. You talk to him," she said as she moved out of the cord's reach. I tried everything, even tossing a magazine at her from the counter in an attempt to get her to come to the phone, but she wouldn't budge. I was trapped.

"Michael, Dalia's in the back doing something that really can't wait. She should be done soon, though," I said as I narrowed my eyes and curled my lips at her. "She asked me to talk to you until she's finished. You don't mind, do you?"

"No, of course not. Norma, does Dalia say anything about me? I mean, I know we don't know each other very well, but has she ever even mentioned me?"

"She's mentioned you."

"What does she say? I mean . . . I really like her. I feel as if I've known her for a long time. I just want to talk to her, be with her, you know what I mean. It's strange, I've seen thousands of women, but I've never felt anything like the emotions I felt when I first saw her three months ago."

Though I had no experience with romantic relationships, his clarity about his feelings didn't strike me as unusual. Arab culture is so structured and formal that men often choose their partners based on a glance. Michael's instant attraction to Dalia seemed normal, even if this confessional flood did not. Could my brothers have said these things so freely? And it still nagged in my mind that he had waited three weeks. Why? Yet I knew that if Michael and Dalia shared the same religion, his next step would have been to ask her father for her hand in marriage. They would then have had the opportunity to get to know each other through chaperoned visits.

"Dalia claims that she felt the same way toward you," I said.

"Oh, that's such a relief. You have no idea how many nights I've stayed awake wondering if she felt anything for me."

I plunged on, hardly able to believe my own forwardness. I think the three of us had been so bottled up, so ready to explode with tension, that this chance to talk was like a dam bursting. "Well, I don't know exactly what you two plan to do about it.

She's Muslim and you're Catholic. If you were Muslim, you could ask for her hand, but as it is, you can't. I can see that you both want to see each other. But why would you want to invite all the problems and, maybe, some hurt that *nothing* can come of it?" By this point, though, I already knew I would be playing the matchmaker as events unfolded. It was clear that the feelings between them were not only deep, they were mutual. So I found myself acknowledging to Michael, "I've promised to do all that I can to help her."

"I know the dangers, but I'm willing to risk it. Is she? I don't care that she's Muslim, she could be Buddhist and it wouldn't matter to me or change my mind."

"I feel the same way you do about religion, as does Dalia, but her parents are more traditional and won't understand. She's willing to risk it, though."

"We can worry about that later. First we need to figure out how we can see each other. Do you think I could come to the salon?" he asked.

Looking back, I see that this was the moment when I should have paused and reflected. Whatever I answered would be the beginning, the first act, of a conspiracy I could scarcely imagine being part of. This was the moment when I should have been suspicious of his garrulousness, of why he'd waited three weeks—of why, if he loved her, he could care so little about the risk he was putting her in. He was Arab—he knew the code, the dangers. We all did.

Yet I realize, looking back, that I trusted his confidence. Coming from a long line of military men, he was trained from birth to win not just battles, but anything he attempted. He was not trained to face the possibility of losing. I knew he'd probably traveled and been schooled abroad, lived in freer cultures where women were not crushed, where honor crimes did not exist. Just talking to him made me feel our prison was a little less inevitable, our risks a little less real . . . but what if his emotions had blinded him to some of the dangers? Or if he was fooling himself that Jordan had progressed beyond the primitive codes in his absence?

Maybe we were all naive. But as I talked with Michael, I was sharing what Dalia felt from the first; I could feel our dreams, our stifled rebelliousness, being fanned into fire by his optimism and strength. I didn't have it in me to deny either of them this chance at being together. And part of me was drawn in by the thought of living this dream vicariously.

"Did you say *you* come to the salon? That's out of the question. Her brother Mohammed, the one who walked in as you and Jehan were leaving, is here every day. He comes and goes as he pleases so we never know when we'll be alone."

"Well, what if you and Dalia befriended my sister? We could see each other through her. Jehan and I are very close, and she's willing to help me. I've already told her how I feel about Dalia."

"That might work. Let's see. . . . It would take time, though, and Mohammed would have to see her here a lot before he'd trust her to take us anywhere. Is she very busy?" I asked.

"Don't worry, she can juggle things if she has to. She's staying in school so my father doesn't force her into an arranged marriage, as he did to my other sisters."

"Really? Are your sisters older or younger than you?"

"They're younger and what he did to them is terrible. Aida is twenty-eight and has a beautiful two-year-old daughter, Jasmine. Her husband's okay, he's not a *hakeer* [jerk] or anything, it's just that he wasn't her choice and she's not in love with him. She loves her little girl, though; I don't think I've ever seen a more devoted mother. She has a nursing degree, but her husband won't let her work. Now she feels as if it was all a waste of time. My sister Miriam is only twenty-three, and my father made her marry a forty-six-year-old *fus* [fart] instead of continuing with school. She cried for days when my father forced her to stop going to school. She wanted to become an English professor."

As he rattled on, nonstop, about his family, I could still hear nervousness in his voice. I hadn't expected this kind of open, detailed description of his family. But he made it easy to keep the conversation going while we waited for Dalia to find enough courage to come to the phone. I was nervous, too, and thankful that he was doing most of the talking. It was rare and refreshing to hear a man being sensitive to his sisters' lives, and daring to be critical of other men.

"I'd love to meet Miriam. I went to English schools, but rarely have the chance to speak English anymore," I said.

"No such luck. The *hakeer* she's married to hardly lets her visit us, much less go anywhere else."

"Well, I guess that's life, here at least. Since Dalia and I are the only girls in our families, our mothers need us to help out at home and so we haven't been forced into marriage yet."

"That's the only thing saving Jehan. That and my mother's failing health. She isn't physically ill, or at least no one has diagnosed her illness. I think my father's tyranny has worn her down over the years. He's a very stern and controlling man. He spent most of his life in the armed forces and treats my mother like one of his recruits—always yelling at her and cutting her down. The whole thing makes me so angry. I wish I could get her away from him.

Oh, let's talk about something else; this is too depressing. Obviously, I don't come from a model family, but then who does?"

"Well, every family has its secrets." By now, I felt enough courage to get flip, joking to lighten the tone of our conversation. "Hey, I have an idea, since you're Catholic and I'm Catholic, maybe you could set me up with one of your brothers. Dalia said you have two, then we'd be related. If that happened, you could see Dalia all the time." Michael took me seriously.

"Oh, you don't want to get involved with them. Jerius is younger than me, but has been married for four years. He has two young sons, and sometimes I really think that he's trying to raise them to be the next Arab Hitlers. But instead of targeting Jews, he's teaching them to target women. It's a pity, really, because his wife, Samia, is so gentle, quiet, and kind. She never smiles, though. I guess I wouldn't smile if I had to deal with Jerius. She reminds me of my mom. I think that's how my mother must have been at her age."

"What about your other brother?" I asked, more out of curiosity than anything else.

"George? He's twenty-five, and the picture of male beauty—but that's where his perfection ends. I hate to say it, but he's very shallow, vain, and arrogant—and very everything you wouldn't want to spend the rest of your life with. He's a typical young Arab man who is financially successful and expects everyone to treat him as if he's a god. I think he might actually try to force his wife to give up her religion and worship *him*. You wouldn't want to be the lucky woman, would you?"

"No, no, no! I don't want that! Michael, can you hang on a minute? I've just realized that I should go check on Dalia. You two should talk before we have to hang up. Hold on," I said, as I put the receiver on the front counter. Mohammed would be here soon. I walked over to Dalia, who'd been listening to my end of the conversation, and physically dragged her to the phone.

"What's wrong with you, Dalia? First you can't wait to talk to him, and now he's on the phone and you won't even pick it up! He sounds really nice and he's dying to talk to you. He's rambled on and on, just as nervous as you are." I covered the receiver with my hand, and snapped in a loud stage whisper, "Now, take this call!"

"All right, all right, just give me a minute," she said.

"You've had at least thirty minutes to get ready—enough!"

She ran to the phone and picked it up, and I left the room so she could have some privacy. I went into the break room and made a fresh pot of coffee just as Mohammed burst in and plopped himself down on the couch, waiting for us to serve him. Dalia hung up swiftly when she saw him, but we'd have no chance to sit and go over our conversations with Michael. We could hardly bear it.

"I told the guys I'd meet them at seven, and I need to pick up Khaldoun before that." He was pushing us, insisting we cancel our seven o'clock appointment to speed his getaway.

"With our regular customers during the week and wedding parties on the weekends for the next three weeks, when else will we fit her in?" But it was futile. He was dashing off to pick up some things for his big night, and knew we'd cancel our seven o'clock to accommodate his silly plans.

"Norma, get me some coffee." Never any "please" from this idiot. I fumed that I had to kowtow to him, but before he left I'd at least try to seize the moment to further our secret plans.

"Since we've been so busy and have all these bridal party bookings coming up, well, Dalia and I have been thinking that it might be wise to hire a girl, a student or something, to help out a bit.

You don't think your father would have a problem with that, do you? I've discussed it with my father and he doesn't. We just need a shampoo girl, or someone to help with the cleanup a few hours a day," I said.

"I don't see a problem. I'll ask him tomorrow and see what he says. Anything else?"

"Actually, yes . . . If your father agrees, you should know that we already have a candidate in mind. She's a nice girl, a student, who's about twenty-one or two. She can juggle her schedule to accommodate ours. If you let me know tomorrow, then I'll give her a call."

"Okay, I'll talk to my father tonight," he said, as he swallowed his last sip of coffee and left.

Dalia and I stayed in the break room, but we needed to focus on Jehan, not Michael.

"Why did you tell Mohammed we wanted to hire a shampoo girl?" she asked, a bit shocked.

"I'm just setting the stage for Jehan's arrival. She's his sister, by the way," I said, not knowing whether Michael had told her. We'd still had no time to talk.

Her shoulders slumped with relief and a smile spread across her face. "I figured she must be. Are you sure she can spend that much time here?"

"According to Michael, she can and will rearrange her schedule to help the two of you." There were now four of us in on The Plan. We must start thinking creatively, and with an espionage agent's attention to detail. We were terrified of being caught, and must miss nothing. First, we must free ourselves more from Mohammed.

"It looks as if Mohammed has snapped out of his rut. Let's

pray that he'll go back to his regular routine and we'll have our break room to ourselves again! I've been going nuts since he started hanging out here every day. We should convince him to take up an activity," I suggested. "That would keep him out of our hair even longer."

"I don't think there's anything else he could possibly do on that dumb truck of his. How about a class or something?" she suggested.

Yes. But what? I had it—weightlifting!

"We could persuade him to build up his muscles," I said. "Tell him how wonderful he's looking, what a noticeable difference it's making. Oh, I can see it now; he'd live at the gym—if we could convince him to go there." We both thought furiously. "We'd buy him a membership. Give it to him as a gift. And tell him we did it because he's been feeling so down lately, and we wanted to help," I said, completing the plot.

"You're a genius!"

But would it work? Mohammed would be back soon. We rushed to cancel the last appointment and clean up, not daring to ponder how typical and pathetic an example this was of what our society forced us to do—serving the whims of this guy like slaves while plotting to manipulate him so that we could have our tiny taste of freedom and excitement.

This was Thursday night, men's night out in Amman. Friday is the Muslim day of worship, when everything's closed.

"What do you think they do all night?" I asked.

"Well, Selma says they go to secret places where they see women dance and do other things."

"But no woman is allowed out that late."

"Not Arab women, foreigners!"

"I don't believe it. You know how Selma is, she hears one little thing, and turns it into headline news. I think they just sit around and play backgammon or cards and smoke their *argilas* and talk."

"I overheard the twins once, when they were getting ready to go out, say that they were going to miss some show called *Baywatch* that some club picks up on its TV. It's an Israeli show or something. Maybe they just watch foreign shows all night."

Mohammed's pickup roared up the street and came to an abrupt stop outside the salon. He leaned on the horn until Dalia ran out to see what was wrong. An instant later she returned with instructions to close up immediately and get into the car; Mohammed was already late. We left everything as it was and ran out to the pickup. Mohammed was impatient and irritable. He hollered at us to hurry in and close the doors, and then he sped off, almost hitting another driver.

Every Thursday, most of the men in both of our families, like most of the men in Amman, rushed home from work and got ready to go out. Many went to one of the several sleazy bars in downtown that are tucked away in the maze of alleys around the Cliff and Venecia hotels. Amman's only other bars or discos are inside the larger hotels such as the Marriott or the Hyatt, where younger night dwellers go.

At night Amman transforms into a strange world. When I was around four or five, my father would take me to the city center at night. I had to wait in the car while he ran in to pick up *sahlab* (a traditional milk drink served warm with nuts and cinnamon) for me. I remember that the streets were full of men, both young and old. Some were seated at outdoor cafés, smoking water pipes and drinking mint tea. Older men gathered in large groups on the street corners, dressed in the traditional long *dishdashay*, while the men of our generation preferred the "American style," jeans and a dress shirt, or the "English style," replacing the jeans with dress slacks.

Whatever in their dress, men have varied options open to them, unlike women. They can make their own decisions, choose their own careers, decide whether or not to marry (though most marry when asked to by their fathers), select their own hobbies and activities, and decide whether to remain at home or move out. Men in a Muslim society are free to do as they wish within the guidelines laid out by their religion.

Different laws ruled Dalia. You'd see her on the street and, if you were Jordanian, you'd instantly know the Muslim laws that ruled her and her body. Her graceful body would be sheathed in the long, loose folds of her *shar'ia*, and her hair hidden by her veil. Dalia has worn the *shar'ia* since she was ten, which for women is the beginning of adult life. The tradition of child-woman is at least as old as Mohammed himself. Islam's founder was married to an even younger child, six-year-old Aisha, and consummated the marriage sexually when she was nine. Aisha was only one of Mohammed's many child brides.

Dalia and I became friends at an age when she was not yet required to follow all of these regulations and customs, and we loved each other as sisters before we reached the age when the rules could have influenced our feelings toward one another and divided us. Her family allowed her to continue her friendship with me, most likely because we both lacked sisters and because they never thought it would develop into such a close union. When, at ten, she was forced to obey the regulations set for adult women, together we found ways for her to tiptoe around them and, temporarily at least, escape some of the restrictions. But as a Christian, I was bound by my own set of rules—and many were the same as hers.

By our early teens, Dalia and I had learned how to navigate this treacherous religious landscape, even if we hated it. So far we had survived. But, with Michael on the scene, look how we were now being forced to behave. How could we be proud of such petty and demeaning behavior? How could two intelligent, middle-class women pay such slavish obedience to a shallow young brother? How could we rely on subterfuge and manipulation to get what we wanted, and let a gossipy neighborhood beauty salon define the boundaries of lives that could have been much bigger? How could we risk our lives simply for a romance?

It is only now, looking back six years from the beginning of our dangerous adventure—years of experiencing freedom, traveling oceans, continents, and cultures—that I can see that our actions would be incomprehensible to women of any liberated culture. As incomprehensible as the violent acts against non-Muslims, non-Arabs, that, since September 11, 2001, have made the Western world suddenly hungry to understand this alien place. They read scholars, watch TV pundits. How much more they would learn if they had lived for a day in our shoes, in Amman, in our neighborhood, in our salon. Then they would understand the forces that wrote Jordan's history, and our personal histories. They would begin to glimpse the laws that dictate the shape of every moment of every day of the ordinary lives of people like Dalia and me, and our families.

And don't be deluded by Mohammed's freedom to wear blue jeans and go to a bar. *Both* sexes are bound by the thousands of rules that carpet Jordan and the Middle East with a dense tapestry of overlapping and interwoven layers of Muslim, Arab, Christian, and Jewish codes and traditions, all of it dominated by the pervasive power of the Koran, Islam's holy book and manifesto. The difference, of course, is that if men break any of these rules, they are to be forgiven. Women's limitations are harder to list simply because the list is continually being expanded and edited by both male lawmakers and the men in a woman's own family. And if a woman breaks any of the rules she's required to follow, she is not granted the luxury of forgiveness. She must be punished.

SEVEN

Violence is embodied in our laws and in our history. It applies to warriors in battle, to perceived enemies of Islam, to Muslims who try to escape the faith, and, above all, to women. Listen to these words from Islam's holy book, the Koran. This passage is the source of the honor killing—the legal murder—of women:

"Men are in charge of women, because Allah hath made the one of them to excel the other, and because they spend of their property (for the support of women). Good women are obedient, guarding in secret that which Allah hath guarded. As for those from whom ye fear rebellion, admonish them and banish them and scourge them."

In the Arabic text, the last portion of this verse, "scourge them" is often translated to mean "kill them." Arab men believe that this verse orders them to "kill" any female relative who is not obedient, or who shows any sign of rebellious behavior. This act is called an honor killing, or a crime of honor, because the men believe that they must kill the offending woman in order to protect their family's "honorable" name and reputation. This kind of killing rarely makes the papers. It is kept out of the civil justice system. But it happens routinely, even today.

Since most Arabic countries have been under Islamic law since A.D. 644, honor killing is no longer considered just an Islamic practice. It has been incorporated into Arab culture and is practiced by both Christians and Muslims, embracing both Dalia and me (for my blood is Arab). And in Arab culture, an entire family's reputation is tied to the reputations of its female members.

It is this codified obsession with honor that drove Dalia's brother Mohammed to guard and watch us like a jailer. It is what would permit him, or any of our brothers or fathers, to literally drive a dagger into our hearts if we betrayed whatever they perceived as honor.

We can lay the violence that has been part of the Islamic culture for nearly fourteen hundred years at the feet of another Mohammed. Since Mohammed's followers took Mecca by force, the first *jihad* in Muslim history, the story of Islam has been filled with wars and bloody battles. I've never found it surprising that a religion founded by vicious warriors and scarred by centuries of bloodshed contains such endorsements of violence, and then wraps it in the dignity of "honor"—and of law—without a qualm.

It is safe to say, I believe, that Islam is a totalitarian regime operating under the guise of a religion. The Koran is its manifesto, claimed by Islam to provide guidance for all that is needed for a person's spiritual and physical well-being. It tells Muslims when and how to have sex and when and how to refrain from it, what to possess and what to give away, when to sleep and when to wake, when to speak up and when to remain silent, what and how to eat and to dress, and how to seek knowledge. It shows Muslims how to deal with the world around them; outlines the responsibilities of a person to himself, to his parents, siblings, offspring, spouses, neighbors, society, and nation; details what habits to cultivate and what to avoid. In short, Islam contains laws and restrictions covering every aspect of life, controlling you from birth to death. And, if you are born Muslim, there is no escape. It is against Muslim law to convert from Islam to any other religion—such a conversion is punishable by death.

There are six basic daily rules that neither men nor women can escape. One is the ritual they must follow prior to performing their prayers: washing their hands, arms, feet, face, and neck, then facing Mecca. The other five rules are known as the "Five Pillars of Islam." *Sala* is the obligation of prayer, which should be performed five or six times a day. *Haj*, which is considered the pinnacle of a devout Muslim's life, is the pilgrimage to the holy sites in and around Mecca, usually performed in the last month of the Muslim year, *Zuul-Hijja. Zakat*, or giving alms to the poor, are various forms of tax that should been paid through the years and is a vital part of Islamic social teaching.

Sawm, fasting, is also known as Ramadan and is celebrated in the ninth month of the Muslim calendar, and commemorates the revelation of the Koran to Mohammed. It is a month that tests human discipline. During this month, all Muslims are required to abstain from sex and from letting anything pass through their lips from dawn to dusk, including water and cigarettes. It is against the law to be seen eating or drinking outdoors during the day, regardless of your religion. Finally, *Shahada* is the profession of the faith and is the basic tenet of Islam: *"La illaha illa Allah Mohammed rasul Allah"* (there is no God but Allah, and Mohammed is the prophet).

Since Jordan is a Muslim country, it is not surprising that although I am not a member of that religion, my family and I had to live according to their law. In the world of Islam, Christian and Jewish inhabitants of a Muslim country are referred to as *dhimmah* (the protected minority). We are not an enemy exactly, but closely watched second-class citizens. Living protected as a *dhimmah* does not come free. According to Islamic law non-Muslims must meet five conditions. First, they must pay the *jizyah*, a poll tax, in order to protect their rights. Next, they must not harm Muslims, have any sexual engagement with Muslim women, steal the property of Muslims, nor cooperate with the enemies of Islam. The list goes on. We non-Muslims must not be flagrant with prohibited things, such as intoxication, adultery, and incest. We must not build new churches or temples, or sound church bells. We must not build any building taller than one belonging to a Muslim, as this would disgrace our neighbors.

If we break the rules, violence is evoked. Non-Muslims who break the conditions of their protection are considered *muharib* (hostile), justifying the declaration of a *jihad* (holy war) against them. Muslims are *required* to fight if they believe that non-Muslims have rebelled against the law. They are taught to take up the sword and advance to the point that non-Muslims, fearing for their lives, say, "We are Muslims" or "We will retain our own religion, and will carry on our own way of worship, but we will publicly follow the laws of Islam." If this capitulation happens then the non-Muslims are once again *dhimmah* and therefore safe. If, however, they refuse to state this, then Muslims must "cleanse the world of [the non-Muslims'] existence" in order to preserve Islamic society and maintain the integrity of the faith.

The Koran, the Muslim holy book, refers to the early prophets of the Bible and the Torah, but that's where the similarities end. Muslims believe that the Koran is the literal word of God as it was communicated to Mohammed in a series of revelations during the early seventh century. Mohammed was born in Mecca in modern-day Saudi Arabia in A.D. 570 and began receiving revelations in A.D. 610. He moved to a nearby town in 622 because the powerful families of Mecca had grown increasingly outraged by his claims. This migration, or *Hejiri*, marks the beginning of the Islamic calendar. His followers returned to Mecca in 630 and took it by force, the first *jihad* in Muslim history. By 644, Muslims had taken Jordan, Egypt, Syria, Iraq, Lebanon, and Israel and spread into North Africa, Spain, and France. I admit that Christianity's hands also drip with blood. But from the first *jihad*, Islam's history is one of wars and death in the name of the faith.

The Islamic legal code is divided into two parts: *ibadat* and *mu' amilat*. *Ibadat* (the intention of intimacy with God) is required of all Muslims. *Hajj*, prayer, fasting, almsgiving, good deeds, prevention of evil deeds, and, finally, *jihad* are all considered *ibadat*. And here, again, the call to war and violence is embedded and codified. There are rules about how these acts should be performed, and for what reasons. For example, if a man grabs a sword and sets off to fight disbelievers without doing so for the pleasure of God, he will not be rewarded, but if he does so with "divine intention," then he is considered *shuhada* (a model) for the entire community and will be rewarded by God. In the Koran, whenever there are the commands *qatilu* (wage war) and *jahidu* (struggle), there is also the order *fi sabil Allah* (strive in the way of God). Muslims claim that Islam is the true religion because it has not disregarded the necessity of warfare.

The other side of the Muslim code, *mu'amilat*, focuses on interpersonal relations—on private lives—and contains laws instructing and regulating every possible aspect of life, including how to appoint a *Mujtahid* (a jurist who must be male and is the equivalent of a judge); what type of water (faucet, rain, or well water) is permissible for personal use, for cooking, and for washing; which types of soaps or gels are acceptable, and which are prohibited; and even how and when to use the lavatory, and the correct way to clean yourself afterward. It lists things that are considered *najis* (evil, unclean) and explains how to make them *pak* (acceptable and clean), or warns how to avoid them. It is this section of the law that states that a non-Muslim is *najis*, and should be avoided, that was relevant to Dalia and me as Michael entered our lives. If contact is unavoidable, for example, if a Muslim is forced to shake the hand of a non-Muslim in business dealings, the code lists the steps a Muslim must follow to cleanse himself of this taint of evil.

A woman's every move is well covered by *mu'amilat*. There are rules for marriage, divorce, sex, sleep, food, death, burial, bank transactions, and the purchase or sale of property and personal items. And, of course, it states that men are superior to women.

Islamic laws make no distinction between Muslim and non-Muslim women. The Jordanian government, however, does distinguish between the two. For instance, non-Muslim women are expected to dress conservatively, covering as much of their bodies as they can, and to avoid tight-fitting clothing. Muslim women, however, must abide by the following much stricter law:

A woman should conceal her body and hair from a man who is non-*Mahram* [unrelated], and as an obligatory precaution she should conceal herself even from a *Na-Baligh* [young] boy who is able to discern between good and evil and could probably be sexually excited, but she can leave her face and hands (up to her wrists) uncovered in the presence of a *Na-Mahram* as long as it does not lead him to cast a sinful evil glance, or to her doing something forbidden; for in both these cases she must cover them.

It is from this law that the *shar'ias* that Dalia would wear were born, the traditional dress, a loose-fitting garment that comes only in colors accepted by Islam, i.e., no bright colors are allowed. It can be worn alone or over clothing and has a high collar, long sleeves, and is long enough, in most cases, to fall just below the ankles. While I could grow up to wear modest skirts and slacks, Dalia had been forced to wear the *shar'ia* since she was ten. While I could wear my hair loose on the street, her veil would cover her head. But once inside the salon, she would change it for a smaller, less shrouding one.

While Christians are allowed to wear cosmetics as long as their fathers permit it, Muslim women are not allowed to use cosmetics or nail polish, except under certain conditions specified by law: a Muslim woman can use cosmetics when it is for the pleasure of her husband, when she is among other women, or when she is among men whom she cannot marry, such as her brother, father, or son. Dalia and I usually dabbled in cosmetics, practicing makeovers on each other, and as long as we did it in private and she removed all traces of the makeup before returning home, it was not forbidden.

In itself, nail polish is not *haraam*—forbidden. However, if it is used during *wudhu* (preparation for prayers) and impedes the flow of water to the fingernails, then it is not allowed. Moreover, if the nail polish is alluring to a non-*mahram*, then it becomes *haraam*.

Islam claims that the Koran specifies all that is necessary for a person's spiritual and physical well-being. It shows Muslims how to deal with the world around them. Since we (Christians) are required to follow their (Muslims') laws, people notice very few differences in our public behavior from that of our Muslim neighbors. Dress, nail polish, and makeup are visible differences. But they are only on the surface. The deeper disparities are only revealed in the privacy of our homes, when we are with our families.

There were differences between my household and Dalia's. Dalia, for example, was never allowed to join her father or brothers for a meal. When they had company, everyone ate at the same time, but the women were in one room, usually with the young children, and the men were in another. My family didn't follow this custom. Men and women were allowed to eat together, but the women were expected to serve the men, and could not begin eating until the oldest male had started. Dalia and I, however, were both expected to cook the meals and clean up afterward, although our mothers usually prepared the evening meal.

Also, there were certain rooms in Dalia's home designated for men, and she was only allowed in them when no men were present, and then only to clean them. Whereas, in my house, we were all allowed to enter every room regardless of whether or not there were men in them. Everyone had to wake up before sunrise in Dalia's house so they could perform their morning prayers. They could return to bed afterward, but only if they got up again before noon prayers. In my home, we were not required to wake up at a particular time, just early enough to meet the demands of the day's schedule.

These small differences between Muslims and Christians were barely noticeable to us, and yet the divide, though not publicly stated, goes much deeper than this. It comes from a deeply held prejudice, imbedded in the heart of the Muslim religion. While the Koran does not specifically state that you must stay away from

Christians, it calls all non-Muslims *unbelievers,* or the unfaithful. Woven into many of its passages are phrases and comments declaring the superiority of Islam over Judaism and Christianity, in particular, and suggesting that faithful Muslims should avoid personal relationships with members of those religions:

> Oh ye who believe! Take not for friends unbelievers rather than believers. . . .

> They desire that you should disbelieve as they have disbelieved, so that you might be [all] alike; therefore take not from among them friends till they forsake their homes in the way of Allah, but if they turn back then seize them and kill them wherever you find them and take not from among them a friend or helper.

This is the passage that gave birth to the rule that if anyone tries to leave Islam and convert to another religion, he or she shall be put to death:

> Those who believe do battle in the cause of Allah, and those who disbelieve do battle for the cause of Evil; so fight ye against the friends of Satan [minions of the devil].

In this verse we (all nonbelievers) are referred to as friends of Satan. Had Dalia and her family honored this rule, we would never have been friends.

Bigotry, discrimination, and male chauvinism are not just implied in Islam, they are an integral part of Muslim law. It is a religion that caters to men's desires and demands the total submission of women. This prejudice was at the root of the laws that made a relationship between Dalia and Michael a crime. It was the laws governing man—woman relationships and marriage that would determine the fate of their budding romance.

There was even a stipulation that would have kept Dalia and Michael from getting to know each other without secrecy and sub-terfuge, even if they had both been Muslims. Following the rules that apply to both Muslims and Christians, dating was impossible for either religion. Although it is not specifically banned, if you abide by all of the Koran's laws you'd have to break several laws in order to date. For example, it is *haraam* (prohibited) for a man and woman who are not *Mahram* (related) to be together if no one else is present, as it could lead to immorality and scandal. Over the years, this law has grown to mean that a woman is not allowed anywhere in public or private with a non-related male; she must always be accompanied by a male relative. So when a woman is seen entering a public place, people assume that the man escorting her is a relative; it is rare to see any women around town unaccom-panied by a male, especially in the evening. If you do spot one or two single women, you can be sure they are either tourists or mod-ernized Christians, though most Christian households have yet to advance that far. Certainly not mine.

But even if Dalia and Michael had surmounted the challenge of getting to know each other, the old prejudices so infected the laws of marriage that the barriers could never be climbed.

A spontaneous romance—the Western idea of marriage for love—defied the old practice of arranged marriage, another tradi-tion that can be traced back to the time of Mohammed's marriage to a child, Aisha, which was arranged by her grandfather. The laws governing arranged marriages are very clear:

If a person proposing marriage is known for his virtue and faith, then it is recommended that his proposal should not be rejected. The Prophet is reported to have said: "Whenever you receive a proposal for marriage to your daughter from a man whose virtue and piety pleases you, then give him her hand in marriage. For if you do not do this way, great scandals and lapses will fill the earth."

Arranged marriages can either be temporary or permanent, and can be arranged by either a grandfather or a father, but not by a brother. Although most arranged marriages occur in Muslim households, all Arabs follow this tradition. Many families claim that they allow a woman to make the final decision about her marriage, but this is just not so. In truth, if a woman decides that she doesn't want to marry a certain man, a verse from the Koran is invoked, which ultimately voids her decision and leaves the final choice up to her father. The verse states that one should fear his parents in the same way one would fear a cruel king, and that one should give priority to their desires over his own. In essence, a father only has to state that it is his desire for her to marry a certain man, and she is required to oblige.

In Jordan, the laws that apply to marriage were a minefield of dangers for Dalia and Michael. For instance, a Muslim woman cannot marry a non-Muslim man, and a Muslim man cannot permanently marry a non-Muslim woman who is not *Ahlul Kitab* (Jewish or Christian). There are certain sects, such as Khawarij, Ghulat, and Nawasib, who claim to be Muslim, but who are classified as non-Muslims. Muslim men and women cannot contract a permanent or temporary marriage with them. In essence, a Muslim man can marry a non-Muslim woman, but a Muslim woman does not have the same privilege. Muslims believe that children are the property of the father, since they carry his name. If a Muslim male marries a non-Muslim female, his children are still Muslim. However, if a Muslim woman marries a non-Muslim man, her children would belong to her non-Muslim husband, and so the union is prohibited.

At least Michael and Dalia would never have to live—at least in Jordan—with the laws that governed women once they were married, when another set of laws outlined their duties as a wife and mother. It is *haraam* for a married woman to go out of the house without her husband's permission. She must also submit herself to her husband's sexual desires and should not prevent him from having intercourse with her without a justifiable excuse. As long as she does not fail in her duties, her husband is required to feed, clothe, and house her. However, "If the wife does not fulfill her matrimonial duties toward her husband, she will not be entitled for the food, clothes, or housing, even if she continues to live with him."

These laws place women in a no-win situation. Most Muslim women cannot work and so do not have access to their own income. Therefore, in order for a woman to get the things she needs to survive—food, clothing, medicine—she has to obey all of her husband's requests and demands, or else he doesn't have to feed her. In reality, these laws mean that if a woman wishes to live, she must obey.

And so in this stifling climate of laws, a modest beauty salon in Amman became the stage for an epic struggle between the almost blinding force of Islam and a fragile *haraam*—forbidden—love.

EIGHT

Jehan joined the conspiracy on the twenty-third day of the sixth month, known as June or AKA (Huzayrān) by Arabic or Islamic calendars. That was the day she began coming to the salon. She had completed her semester of classes at Jordan University and was now on summer break.

By June, Jordan begins to feel like an airless furnace, with temperatures starting at 86 degrees Fahrenheit and steadily climbing until they have reached well into the high 90s. Jordan is an arid country, with an annual rainfall somewhere below 200 millimeters. The many wildflowers that blanket the fields in the valley Wadi as-Seer, near Amman, begin to shrivel in the grueling heat and shortage of water. Hummus season starts, and vendors set up all along streets and highways selling roasted hummus—green chick peas roasted in an open flame while still in their soft shells and attached to the stem—by the stem or by the kilo.

In Jordan, the wedding season was in full swing, and a salon hairstyle on the wedding day was a ritual for all the women in a bridal party. This year, as for the past five years, Dalia and I were run off our feet, and refused most of our regular appointments to focus on wedding parties. Arab wedding ceremonies are very colorful and noisy affairs. The celebrating begins the night before, when all the men drive or march down the streets in a convoy, singing and dancing, while the women, dressed in their best clothes, go to the bride's home for a night of their own singing and dancing.

That evening the women are allowed to remove their veils, since no men are present. It is one of the only times in a woman's life when she feels comfort, ease, and freedom.

On the morning of the wedding day, the men again gather and begin their noisy procession to the bride's home to escort her to the mosque, or to the church if the couple are Christian. This is where the similarities between Christian and Muslim weddings end. At a Muslim wedding, men and women are separated during the reception. The groom is allowed to join the women long enough to dance with his bride once, after which he must return to the room designated for men. But Christian receptions take place in the same room, with men and women celebrating together.

The bride-to-be chooses a salon to go to on her wedding day with all the women in her bridal party, including the flower girl. They have their hair styled and their makeup applied. Most wedding parties would come to our salon, but some preferred to have us come to the bride's home. As a result, our schedule was often very hectic during these months. The group usually consisted of at least ten women, and we had to style all of them in a three- to four-hour period. Our calendar was booked for the next three months, so, since we truly needed Jehan's help, her arrival at the salon didn't raise any suspicions. Phase one of our communication network was now successfully in place.

To implement phase two, we had to find a way to get Mohammed out of the salon more often. This was not easy and we spent several weeks plotting to put it into effect. The concentration the planning took kept our minds a little bit off our fear of being caught, but it was always there. We thought of many different ideas, playing each scenario out in our minds, always finding some fault or obstacle, and going on to the next. We had to be careful or Mohammed would suspect that we were up to something. Our final choice ended up being our first; we would find a way to enroll Mohammed in weightlifting classes at Sports City, minutes from both our homes and the salon.

First, Jehan asked Michael to buy magazines and books about exercise and weight training. We left them lying around the salon in places we knew Mohammed would see them. Once we saw him reading the magazines and books, we knew it was time for step two. Dalia and I started talking, in Mohammed's presence, about the exercises we'd supposedly begun doing and mentioned that they increased our strength and energy. After a week, he began asking us questions. We knew we had him hooked. We gently urged him to try some of them himself. Oh, if only we had access to weights and weightlifting machines, how much better our results would be, we said, nudging him toward joining a health club. It was time for step three.

The next morning we phoned Sports City to discuss a gift membership for our brother, and, with Jehan's help, arranged to have Michael drop off the money for fees and pick up Mohammed's card later that evening.

The next morning we wrapped up all of our workout books and magazines, along with Mohammed's new Sports City membership card, and presented him with his gift when he arrived that afternoon. He was thrilled.

Our plan appeared to have worked perfectly. With Mohammed

at the gym during the day, Dalia and I were free to find more ways to communicate with, and eventually see, Michael.

We were savoring our first small taste of success at manipulating and deluding men—clearly, the only route, for millennia, to any kind of power for Arab women. It gave us a little confidence, subdued the fear a bit. But it felt bittersweet; had we lived in a freer world, it would not have been our strategy of choice.

Through Jehan, Dalia and Michael were able to exchange letters and have short conversations on the phone. Dalia and Michael's letters slowly progressed from one page "I just met you and don't want to reveal too much of me yet" notes to ten-page "I'm pouring my heart and soul out on paper" missives discussing their opinions, beliefs, likes, dislikes, etc. I believed that if this friendship lasted, they would already know more about each other than most Jordanian couples do who have spent their lives together.

Dalia and I quickly became good friends with Jehan and discovered that we had a lot in common. It turned out that Jehan wasn't as quiet as I'd originally thought. She rambled on and on, hopping from one subject to another without taking time to draw a breath. Dalia and I loved her. It was wonderful to meet another woman who shared our beliefs, hopes, and opinions about women's positions and rights. But it would still be months before Mohammed trusted Jehan enough to leave the three of us unaccompanied outside the salon. It would be weeks before Dalia could see Michael again. For now, though, she survived on the letters and sporadic calls.

In fact, everyone was satisfied with the arrangement. Mohammed was ecstatic with his new pastime, had managed to make a horde of new friends at the gym, and was out of our hair from morning until siesta. He was happy to drop us off at the salon or a bride's home and leave. Dalia was thrilled to be in touch with Michael. And we'd found a great friend in Jehan.

But eventually Jehan was going to have to return to school and wouldn't be able to spend much time at the salon. We'd miss her— she had become like a sister to us. Without her here to cover Dalia's calls to Michael, and deliver long letters to him, we needed a new way for the two to communicate. Dalia would only write to him, we agreed, on the days Jehan came in and could courier the letters swiftly home. With classes and her duties at home, Jehan would be here much less. But Dalia and I were sure that we would find a way to persuade Mohammed to take us to see her.

We knew that all this scheming was dangerous, but we never discussed it. It was as if we would give life to the risks if we spoke them aloud. So they remained thoughts and fears that we could successfully blot out while we hatched our plot.

NINE

We became fixated on Fridays, the holy day, when everything in Amman is closed—stores, the salon. Looking desperately for a way to escape our daily prison so that Dalia and Michael could have moments together, we made Fridays our target, our only possible window of opportunity. Dalia and I had always spent Friday evening together, at her home or mine. But that had to change; Dalia would explode if she didn't see Michael soon.

Our first idea was to open the salon Friday afternoons, make that our excuse to be out of the house. The idea died as both fathers opposed it. We refocused our energy on Friday evenings. We needed to find a way to get out. Where could we get Mohammed—or any of our brothers—to drop us off and collect us later without betraying the plan?

Football—soccer to Americans—killed the idea before it was born. Football is Jordan's most popular sport; most of the males in the nation are ardent fans and watch the games religiously every Friday night. As soon as the season began, Mohammed stopped weight training so that he wouldn't miss a game. The chances of getting him to drive us anywhere on Friday evenings during foot-

ball season, which lasted from late September to March, were slim
to none. We searched for another plan.

It was a Thursday night. I could smell the *mahalabiyya*—aromatic
cookies made with rice flour, sugar, milk, and rose water, and
topped with an almond or pine nut—baking from my room,
where Dalia and I were plotting, and I leapt up to dash to the
kitchen. For years we'd been allowed to have a *sihra* on Thursday
evenings—a night when our parents did not impose our usual curfew, and we were allowed to stay up late.

We alternated between Dalia's home and mine. While the cookies baked, we'd make tea and lock ourselves in, playing music as
our cover while we talked through the urgent issues. Days earlier,
we'd had a breakthrough, the only solution: We must find an activity that would require us to be out of the house every Friday afternoon. But what activity? We researched for days, and found it.
Computer classes would be just the thing. Yes! Now we were racking our brains trying to climb the next hurdle: getting our fathers
to agree.

"I don't know if my father will go for something like that, at
least not if I do it alone," I mused. "I think if we did it together,
he'd allow it."

"Your father would at least consider it, but there's no way my
father is going to agree."

"Maybe one of your brothers might convince him that it's
important, and that one of my brothers will be watching us. He'll
listen to one of his sons. I also think we should approach both
fathers at the same time, and make each one believe that the other
has already agreed. That's the only way they'll go for it," I added.

"I don't know, Norma. All they have to do is call each other and
they'll find out we've been lying."

"But what are the chances they'll actually do that? I mean, if we can persuade your brother Suhal to talk to your father, then your father will think that Suhal has already made sure that my father approves of the idea."

For hours, we talked back and forth, on and on. Finally, Dalia said, discouraged, "Maybe it would be better if you just took the class by yourself."

"That won't solve the problem. You want to be able to see Michael and Jehan too, don't you?"

"Of course I do," she said.

We decided we'd call some schools on Monday to find out when their classes meet, then talk to Suhal. If we could lure him to the salon on his way home . . . "Do you really think we can pull this off?" she asked.

"We convinced them that we needed a computer for the salon, so we should be able to convince them that we need computer classes. We already have the computer, and they keep telling us that we wasted our money on it because we hardly use it," I replied.

It was the only solution we could come up with.

"I hope it works." Dalia was clearly worried.

"Don't worry, you'll see. Now let's go eat some *mahalabiyya* before my brothers eat it all."

కిళ

That Monday morning Dalia picked me up for work as usual. September in Amman is a strange mix of winter and summer. The early morning is cold, with occasional bursts of cool winds howling about, the remnants of the frigid desert nights. During the day, the temperatures once again feel as if they are reaching their summer highs. It's as if the transition from summer to winter sneaks in during the night, and the only evidence it leaves behind is the one- or two-degree drop in afternoon temperatures the following day. The cool winds are not strong enough to fight the heat of the summer sun until at least the end of October, leaving September full of sumptuous summer days.

We bought two newspapers on our way to work that day, and searched for advertisements for computer classes. We made a list of all the possibilities, starting with the ones nearest Abdoun, where Michael and Jehan lived.

Our first hair appointment was not until 10:30. That gave us enough time to call those places that morning. We dashed into the break room. I locked the door and switched off the salon lights so we wouldn't be interrupted.

"Do we have enough money saved up to pay for this out of the business account?" I asked. Dalia was our bookkeeper; she'd always had a better head for numbers than I had.

"When I made the deposit last week, we had roughly 7,253 dinars in the bank. That should be plenty," she assured me.

I felt an urgency to get going on the calls.

"Relax, *ya butbouta*, we still have time. Enjoy your coffee and smoke a cigarette, it'll calm you down a little," she said as she tossed a cigarette my way. *Butbouta* literally means duck, but used as slang it implies that someone is acting hyper, in a cute way. Which I was. But we had never planned such a complex violation of the rules, with such risks.

"I'm just excited, aren't you? It's a perfect plan. They'll never guess what we're really up to, and you'll be able to see Michael. We'll even learn a little about computers in the process," I said.

"I don't want to get too excited yet; I'll only be disappointed if it doesn't work," said Dalia, always the more practical of the two

80

of us. Not that she wasn't given to crazy ideas and fantasies, she was just more methodical in implementing them and hid her emotions better than I did. She was my anchor and kept me grounded. I was the only one who ever noticed any slight change in her during critical times, but then again I was the only one who knew all of her secrets.

I ran out to the front desk, with the list of numbers to call clutched tightly in my fist.

❧❧

There were plenty of schools in Shmeisani with beginner classes on Friday and Saturday early evenings, which would be ideal. Our brothers would be watching football when we were supposed to be in class. The tuition was far less than we'd thought it would be. It wouldn't bankrupt us.

Now we had only a few more barriers to get through. First, we had to lure Suhal to the salon on his way home from work, and make him our advocate. Pleading that she wanted his guidance on some urgent matter that had come up, he couldn't deny her appeal; we would call on his duty as older brother to protect and guide her.

An angry mother with a fussy, crying child arrived for a haircut, and our workday officially began.

We worked side by side all morning, barely saying a word and nodding an expected reply here and there in response to a customer's question. Both of us were thinking about what we would say to Suhal. We were trying to figure out how much we should tell him about the classes. We didn't want to say too much because it would make our plan even riskier. The less our families knew the better. We didn't want them calling the school to check up on us.

81

We knew that in order to be successful we had to use a mix of careful preparation, great prudence, and a little audacity.

By two, we were starved, just keeping our minds working so hard. Food! We hurriedly locked the doors and ran to the break room for lunch. I grabbed the container of *maqlubeh* (steamed rice topped with slices of eggplant, meat, tomato, and roasted pine nuts) and tossed it into the microwave, as we started planning our script for Suhal. We rehearsed, edited, and recast our strategy a dozen times in the next half hour.

Suddenly Dalia said, "Norma, let's stop talking about it, it's making me nervous and I don't want to think about it anymore. The more I think about it, the greater chance I'll have of messing up. Let's just eat our lunch in peace."

This was the first time we'd taken such an elaborate risk; we were escalating our conspiracy to a new level, dramatically increasing the chance of being found out. We finished our lunch in silence, each of us afraid to say anything else.

Suhal walked in at 6:15, and as soon as we saw him our insides froze. "*Salem al-laykum* [peace unto you]," he said as he entered. After the greetings, he followed us into the break room where I began making coffee as he and Dalia sat on the couch.

"What seems to be the problem?" he asked Dalia.

"Well, Suhal, I chose to come to you with this because I believe that since you're a teacher you'll understand the importance of this better than the others. You know, Norma and I spent a lot of money on our computer. And, well, we can't operate it well enough to use it properly. Since we've already made the investment in the computer, Norma and her family have decided that it would be wise for her to take some classes at a school in Shmeisani. What do you think?"

"Well, if her family has already agreed to it, then I don't see anything wrong with it. I've never thought you needed a computer in the salon, but now that it's here, she might as well learn how to use it."

"I thought so, too. I was hoping to accompany her to the classes, since we both need to know how to use the computer. Do you think it's wise to consider such a thing? I wanted to get your opinion first, because if you think it's not wise, then I'd rather not bother Dad with it."

"When are these classes? Who will be taking her? When do they start?" he asked. I took that as my cue to join in. I served him coffee, and proceeded to lie more blatantly than I had ever lied in my life. To me, this seemed the point of no return for Dalia and me. If we succeeded with Suhal, the first major physical acts of betrayal would soon begin.

"Suhal, if I may speak, I'll tell you what I know, but since my father has arranged all the details, I'm afraid that all I know is that the classes will be held on Friday and Saturday afternoons. Of course, I must abide by the same curfew as Dalia, and I'm certain that my father has considered that while planning this. Also, one of my brothers will be dropping us off and picking us up. The only time we'll be unaccompanied is while we're in the classroom. I'm certain that my father is placing me in a class of girls. My father will pay the tuition, and I believe that Dalia should also know how to run the computer in case I'm not around. She can maintain all her client information on it. My father thinks it's a shame to let the money we spent on the computer go to waste."

Suhal pondered, taking his role as guardian very seriously. "Well, I don't see any problem with Dalia attending classes with you, and I'll do what I can to get my father to agree. I can speak to my father tonight. To reassure him, I'll offer to take both of you to the school on Friday and enroll you myself. I don't think it'll be a problem."

"Thank you, Suhal. Thank you so much. I knew you'd understand, and I appreciate your talking to Dad on my behalf," Dalia said.

"One down, one to go," she whispered, tidying up to leave. "Are you sure we can convince your dad? Let's say an extra prayer."

I don't think either of us slept that night. I jumped every time the phone rang, thinking it was Dalia's father calling to confirm what Suhal had told him. I felt guilty about the day's deception and hated the idea of repeating it in the morning. I knew that Dalia was struggling with the same emotions.

My father entered the kitchen at his usual hour. I served him his coffee, and began setting the stage for Dalia's arrival.

"Daddy, Dalia and I have something we need to discuss with you. Would it be okay to do it this morning? Will you have time?" I asked.

"Sure, I'll be on the veranda. Bring my breakfast out there," he said as he left the kitchen.

When Dalia arrived we locked ourselves in my room and quickly went over the details of our plan. We managed to suppress our fears while we talked to my father, and in the end he agreed to let me enroll.

There was just one more element to the plan. We didn't want to ask for an escort because then they might find out that we'd lied to them, and so we decided that on the days we had classes, I would ask to walk to Dalia's home, and she would ask to walk to mine. Then we could meet in between and take a taxi to school and back.

Suhal enrolled us in school that Friday and we paid the tuition. The classes would run for the next nine months.

That Monday, we called Jehan and told her our news, and began planning our first meeting for the following Friday. We went over every detail to ensure that we would not be caught and drew up a list of "official ground rules." No one, other than the four of us, could ever know anything about these meetings. We must meet at places none of our families went to. Dalia would remove her *shar'ia* attire during the encounters to look like a Christian girl. In public places Dalia and Michael would refer to each other as brother and sister. Either Jehan or I would always be nearby, to provide cover if needed. And, finally, we must attend some of the classes to show our fathers and brothers that we were learning something.

We planned to meet at the 1001 Nights restaurant in the Le Meridian hotel in Shmeisani for the first outing.

Friday afternoon at 5:00, we left our homes and headed to our meeting point. The moment of truth had arrived and we felt panicked.

We found a taxi quickly, out of sight of all our relatives and nosy neighbors. Sitting in the backseat of the cab, we looked in every direction, double-checking that no one had seen us. We arrived at the school and went into the classroom. Ten minutes into the class, we asked to be excused, saying that we didn't feel well, and went to the rest room. In the bathroom, I took the clothes we'd chosen for Dalia out of my gym bag. She changed and then we walked out of the school, around the corner to Le Meridian hotel, and up to the 1001 Nights restaurant to find Michael and Jehan.

They were sitting at one of the back tables and when we arrived they stood up. Michael's eyes lit up when he saw Dalia, and he had to restrain himself from embracing her. She, on the other hand, blushed, smiled, and lowered her eyes to the floor. With the formalities out of the way, we sat down and began discussing the details of what we still had to do. Then, we enjoyed a tray of mixed desserts and coffee while we talked and laughed, like any group of friends would. For that short time we forgot all our fears and worries, and focused on the fact that we were all together.

During the cab ride home Dalia and I couldn't stop talking about what a wonderful time we'd had, and how amazing it was that something as natural and delightful as an afternoon out with friends was forbidden. As we neared our drop-off point, our anxiety began to build, but this time it was mixed with the satisfaction of having succeeded better than we could have dreamed. With each success, our courage and confidence would grow, with a slight and parallel dilution of our fear. It may have been only pastries and coffee, but this taste of ordinary freedom had been too delicious to stop now. We had traveled just two miles by taxi, but we had entered a different world.

TEN

*I*n the two months following that first afternoon with Michael and Jehan, we managed to arrange six meetings: three at 1001 Nights; two at La Coquette, where we tried genuine French food; and one at La Terrasse, where we heard live music as we ate our pastries. We grew a little more confident with each successful encounter and were having loads of fun. Life was exciting, and we were savoring every moment. We felt freer than we'd ever felt before. We were like children tasting chocolate for the first time, and we couldn't get enough. When we met, Jehan and I chatted, trying to give Dalia and Michael as much privacy as we could.

Later, Dalia and I would explode with the experience. "Norma, this is so incredible. Did you even think that Amman had such wonderful restaurants? They're so beautiful and elegant. Did you see how many people were there? Most of them didn't even speak Arabic. It was like being in a different world."

"I know, it is so wonderful. I'll bet our mothers have never seen anything like them, or even imagined them. I wish we could take them to one of these restaurants."

"Our brothers probably don't even know these places exist. I mean, most of the Arabic-speaking people are employees or Arabs meeting foreigners for business. I hope our brothers never go there, but I would like to share it with our moms."

"And at our first French restaurant, it felt so different, didn't it? No one was watching us, or noticing how we were dressed. Everyone was minding his or her own business. It was great. It made me feel comfortable and free."

"Yeah, although the fact that you were speaking English helped. They probably thought you were foreign and we were entertaining you."

"Oh, come on, I don't look foreign, I look Arabic. I just think that people are more open-minded in those places. Maybe it's because they're used to seeing foreigners."

"Could be. It's not like you and Michael acted like anything more than brother and sister."

"I can't wait until next week. We get to pick the place and set everything up."

We'd told our computer teacher that we could only attend Saturday's classes, explaining that we were the only girls in houses full of men and so had too many household responsibilities on Fridays. Since we'd told him that we were only taking the classes for our personal use, and not for our business skills, he didn't mind if we missed the Friday classes.

I could see that Dalia was falling more and more in love with Michael, and, since the men in our families were busy watching football, we had no reason to think they would check up on us, at least until March. Mohammed had been spending his days with his new friends, so we also had plenty of privacy at the salon.

❧❧

Things became a little more difficult in November, because of the upcoming holidays. November 14 is a public holiday in Jordan celebrating King Hussein's birthday, and Eid al Isra Wal Mi'raj, an Islamic holiday that marks the prophet Mohammed's nocturnal visit to heaven and the visions God revealed to him, immediately follows it. After that, of course, was Christmas. Dalia had a lot to prepare for Eid al Isra Wal Mi'raj. Every year her extended family came together at her home for a night of gift giving and feasting. She had to help her mother with everything, from preparing their home to arranging the menu. She also had to buy gifts for her family, which took up most of her free time. I had to do many of the same things before Christmas, and so the lie we'd told our instructor about Friday classes became true in November and December. During these two months, most of our free time was wasted waiting in checkout lines and fighting through hordes of pushy bargain hunters.

The entire time, our brothers escorted us. We didn't see how we would be able to keep going on our Friday afternoon adventures, but we vowed to try to find a way. We hoped to convince our families to let us keep going to our classes on Fridays, and so we closed the salon on Thursdays in order to have enough time to do our chores. It seemed a reasonable solution, and our fathers let us try it.

After a few weeks, we realized that we'd have to give up some Friday afternoons so we could get everything done. But we didn't waste any time complaining; instead we spent every free second talking about Michael.

"I like a lot of things about Michael," Dalia said one day when we were sitting on the couch in the break room, drinking a cup of hot tea.

"Like what?" I asked.

"Well, for starters, he's absolutely gorgeous, but that's beside the point. What I really like is the fact that he's kind, understanding, and intelligent."

"He does seem to be gentle and kind. What else have you discovered while Jehan and I have been talking?"

"He has a law degree and is planning to become an attorney once he finishes his tour in the Royal Guard. He loves art, like me, and he loves to read. I love the fact that it's so easy to talk to him. I mean there are times when I think we can read each other's minds; we're so much alike. Also, he's traveled, much more than we probably ever will."

"Where's he been?"

"He went to school in London, and traveled to Greece, France, and Italy while he was there. He's fluent in French and even speaks a little Greek and Italian. He's told me about all the different things he's seen and he says that he'd love to show them to me. Apparently we'd be free in those countries and wouldn't have to sneak around to see each other. I would be able to do what I want. Doesn't that sound like heaven?"

"Yes, it does. This whole thing is incredible. I mean, I never thought either one of us would feel like this. Would you marry him if you could?"

"In a second. He's everything I could ever want in a man. I like him a lot, but it's still too soon to say that I love him. I mean, I've never been in love before. I know that I have very strong feelings for him and I think we'd be happy together. He actually *cares* about my opinions, and treats me like an equal."

"That's something he must have learned abroad. They definitely don't teach men that here," I said.

"What does caring about him feel like?" I asked Dalia, entering territory neither of us had ever explored.

Even as best friends, we had never talked directly about what love felt like, and never about sexual feelings, because we didn't know what they were. Sex is not something that is talked about in any context with a single woman in Jordan; we were never taught specifics about sex. For many years Dalia and I thought that if you kissed a man on the lips you would get pregnant. Sex, or the possibility of it happening to a single woman, was thought to be so evil, so horrid, that we were afraid of it. It must seem so strange to a sexually liberated culture; here we were in our twenties, but we didn't feel sexual frustrations or have sexual fantasies, because we were too afraid and didn't really know enough about sex to be able to fantasize about it. In the salon, our married girlfriends would talk to us about it, but what we learned from them was that it was painful, and that you bleed on your first time; things that just scared us more. I have female cousins and aunts older than I who have never married, and are still virgins. That's just the way it is. We were curious and innocent as children.

"Well, it's hard to describe. I get butterflies in my stomach when I think about him. I'm nervous, excited, and happy every time I know I'm going to see him. When I don't see him, I miss him and he's constantly in my thoughts. Even on my bad days, all I have to do is think of him and I start to smile. I can't imagine my life without him."

"You sound as if you're in love. Why do you say you aren't?"

"Because love is something very serious. There's love and then there's being in love, you know. I love you and right now I think that I love him the way I love you. But to be in love with him is a totally different thing, and I don't know if I'm ready for that. I

91

guess what I'm trying to say is that before I could say that I'm in love with him, I'd have to feel sure that I wanted to spend the rest of my life with him and have his children."

"Oh, Dalia, I think you're overanalyzing again. You sound confused. You love him in your heart, but your mind is still trying to evaluate what you're feeling. If I ever fall in love, I want it to be something that I can't analyze but something I just know."

"Norma, you can't decide something this important and serious based on a passing feeling. It's much more complicated than that. You'll know what I mean when you experience it. I could be feeling this way now because I've never disobeyed my parents before. Maybe I have to make him a superhero to justify what I've done. Who knows, maybe I won't feel like this several months from now. All I know is that at this moment he's very, very important to me. He makes me feel things I've never felt before, good things, and I don't want to give that up."

"What do you mean, feel things? What good things?"

Dalia was opening up with a rush of words that reminded me of my first phone call with Michael. The dam was bursting. "He makes me feel special, beautiful, and smart. He respects me, and cares about my wants, needs, and thoughts. He's not like my brothers or my father. I've never seen my father ask my mother for her opinion. He just orders her around and treats her as if she doesn't matter, as if she's just there to serve him. My father treats me the same way. Michael's different; he always asks me things and he listens to what I have to say. My opinion matters to him. Last time we met, he asked me to pick where I want to go the next time. My brothers have never asked me to pick anything. It feels good to be treated as if I'm important."

"My father and brothers are just like yours. As far as they're concerned, women don't have brains, and we're certainly not allowed to have opinions. I hope someday I can find someone who treats me the way Michael treats you. It sounds wonderful. I can't imagine it."

"Oh, Normie, you will. You will find someone like him. You just have to make sure that he's spent a lot of time outside a Muslim country. Try to find someone from one of the countries Michael's been to. He obviously learned those things there."

"Oh, that'll be easy. I'm sure men like Michael are just running up and down the streets of Amman. All I have to do is pick one. Come on, Dalia! You could probably count on one hand the number of men in Jordan who think like Michael. If only he was Muslim, you two could get married."

Then it suddenly hit home, and the euphoria subsided a bit. This was deadly serious. The way this was heading, they would have to leave Jordan. I took Dalia's hand.

"If you ever decide that he's the one you want to have children with, maybe we can find a way for the two of you to be together. I mean, we've been pretty successful so far. We make a great team. Nothing's impossible."

ELEVEN

We survived that holiday season, but we barely had time to see or talk to Michael and Jehan. By now it had been almost one year since Michael and Dalia had met, yet they had really only known each other for five months. We'd spent most of our time figuring out ways for them to communicate. It had been a consuming and exhausting process, but we hoped that as time went on it would become much easier.

Now it was nearing March and we began to realize that as the last of the Muslim holidays were over, they took football season with them. Things were about to get more complicated, not easier. Mohammed would start spending more time at the salon, and our brothers wouldn't be watching games on Fridays; they'd be out in the neighborhood. The risk of one of them spotting us getting in or out of a taxi was much greater. Michael and Dalia were eager to spend more time together and had no interest in discussing the growing risks. But even they couldn't ignore the danger, since it controlled the frequency of their dates.

And even if Michael's military confidence led him to feel immune to defeat or damage, surely he loved Dalia enough to keep in mind the terrible risks to her. But Michael's confidence and worldliness were infectious. We handled the details at this stage with a growing sense of invincibility, and I think we both felt that Michael was capable of making the big things happen—including marriage, and leaving Jordan.

Our objective was clear, and our mission defined: invent and implement a series of covert operations to make it possible for Michael and Dalia to date. We began to feel like military strategists. We started charting, on a neighborhood street map, exactly where we thought our brothers and fathers would be during the crucial hours of the lovers' dates. Several weeks after football season ended, we were nervous wrecks. After achieving every illicit Friday night date, we were a bundle of raw nerves. For the rest of the weekend and the following week, we'd hold our breath, expecting to hear some comment from one of our brothers that he'd seen us the previous Friday. The joy was turning to despair. We were going crazy and realized that we had to search for alternatives.

"I can't sleep for two nights after every meeting. I keep thinking one of my brothers is going to say something like, 'Hey, I thought I saw you and Norma yesterday afternoon.' I can't take it anymore. But I can't stop seeing Michael," Dalia said.

"I know what you mean, I feel the same way. I was thinking that maybe we should have one of them drive us to the school and drop us off. At least that way we wouldn't have to worry about being seen in a taxi," I said.

"That would help, but we'd still have to worry about them spotting us while we're running to the restaurant."

"I know, but at least it would eliminate part of our exposure. I'm sure if we put our heads together, we can think of a way to reduce the other risks as well."

Exasperated after another endless round of examining the pros and cons, I suggested that "We should forget the whole Friday classes thing, and try to get Mohammed to take us to places with Jehan and leave us there for a couple of hours. Now that football season is over, we should be able to get him to do that."

But in the end, we decided to keep to our original plan, as no other method seemed to work as well. For months, we'd been careful to stick to our Thursday schedule in order to avoid making our families suspicious. Each week, we spent hours in my room or Dalia's coming up with ideas and strategies. All of this worry and planning was draining. In the beginning, we thought it would be thrilling, although we'd doubted that it would succeed; by now it had become an obsession to keep the successes going.

Our work at the salon began to suffer as we needed more time to plan and started seeing fewer customers. Not that our families would have disapproved; as far as our fathers and brothers were concerned, the salon was just a way for us to fritter away our time and be together. It wasn't a bona fide business. They never cared about how many clients we had, or how much money we earned. Any cash we made was to be our pocket money, to waste on books and art supplies, decorations, and women's things. Since we weren't married, our fathers and brothers were responsible for all of our basic needs, such as food, clothes, and medicine. We quickly discovered, however, that leading a secret life required money—to buy our brothers gifts or to pay for their activities so they wouldn't discover what we were up to. It was a small price to pay for peace of mind. But we'd have to increase our appointments again.

The money, though, was only a tiny part of the real cost of our activities. We spent hours studying and synchronizing our actions. Since our independence depended on our brothers' schedules, we were forced to quietly alter their activities, all the time convincing them that each new idea came from them and not us. This required a lot of research into our brothers' lives, including their likes and dislikes. As we became masters of manipulation, as we grew better and better at subtly organizing their lives, we felt as if we knew them better than they knew themselves. With most extracurricular activities in Jordan taking place on Fridays and Saturdays, mapping the events to coincide with our trysts was not very difficult. But it drained time. In the end, each glorious afternoon cost hours, and sometimes days, of effort. Dalia was in paradise, often absentminded, so it was my responsibility to check and recheck all the details so that both of us were protected.

It was amazing to see how Michael had changed her. For as long as I could remember Dalia always had a rebellious spirit. As a child, the more she was forbidden to do something, the more she was determined to do it. As we matured and our restrictions grew, the nonconformist within her became deeply resentful of the rules governing her life, and angry with the men who enforced them. But now, her feelings for Michael began to transform her pessimism into optimism. She'd found a man who encouraged and treasured her free spirit. This adventure had reawakened that rebellious child, and she reveled in the excitement. In fact, we inadvertently resumed the same positions we'd played in adolescence. Dalia invented the idea, and I found a way to make it happen.

For days after each date, Michael was our main topic of conversation. It was clear that Dalia was in love with him, although she still refused to admit it. Michael and Dalia had so much in common. Their ideas, political principles, and religious convictions were identical. As a third party looking in, I could easily see the passion their fears blinded them to. But as I had no experience with love, I found myself second-guessing what I believed I saw when Dalia repeatedly talked about the depth of her feelings for Michael. I realized that she was still trying to understand her emotions. Knowing Dalia and our culture, that wasn't surprising; it was expected. I loved watching her twist out of admitting that she was in love. I always knew that Dalia would only use the word "love" when and if she became convinced that it was the only word that could explain what she was feeling. She was too analytical to do anything else; it was one of things I cherished about her.

But if she ever used the word, there would be no turning back from the inevitable next step. I didn't dare think about it. How remarkable romance is in an Islamic country, it occurred to me. All this endless analysis of the depth and destiny of the relationship, and they've never kissed. Never even held hands.

TWELVE

The name Aqaba rings with the romance of Lawrence of Arabia, as he sweeps in to Jordan's strategic (and only) port, and—in full flowing desert robes, riding his camel—seizes it from the Turks, winning the day for the British and their Arab allies, and writing legends for himself.

For Dalia and me, Aqaba rang with a very different meaning. For us, it was the symbol of the battle we lost for our childhoods, a battle that was all over by the time we were nine or ten. Too young to know what was happening, we'd been passive observers of the capture of the free-running freedom we'd known. The victors were our fathers and brothers, and the ancient codes.

It was now May in Amman. The mildest, and often most beautiful, month in Jordan. And Aqaba beckoned as it had every spring since I was a child—the place my and Dalia's families had always gone, and still went, to enjoy Jordan's only seaside resort. Oh, how Dalia and I had loved Aqaba. We believed that the sea held mystical powers and, each year, we'd beg our families to take us there. This year, as Dalia and I searched for a way to avoid joining them, I felt, for a moment, a flash of memory for the freedoms we'd known there when we were small, when we were still little princesses. That was the brief snatch of time where everything we did was cute, and everyone wanted to play with us. How idyllic it looked from the distance of twenty years, the phase when my father was affectionate, when we rough-and-tumbled with our brothers—when we splashed and laughed in the waves at Aqaba, wore a swimsuit or whatever we wished and felt the sun on our sandy young bodies.

It was before the distance grew between me and the father who'd hugged me and held my hand as we hunted for shells. Before my brothers stopped being friends, and turned into guard dogs. At about the time I turned nine, the affection and playfulness stopped. I was then, according to them, turning into a young woman, and young women were expected to dress and act a certain way. With Dalia it was the same, though as a Muslim she had had even stricter rules to live by. Suddenly, we were no longer allowed to run around outside in the neighborhood with other children; the friendly streets were no longer our playground. We were no longer allowed to wear anything we wished; we had to be dressed conservatively.

It became our job at that time to start serving any guests who came over, and cleaning and cooking with our mothers. Our training and preening to become mothers and housewives had begun. As they taught us the domestic skills, our mothers and aunts were teaching us the responsibilities that all women must attend to. They were teaching us to know the primary boundary of our lives: the house. By the time we were eighteen, the emotional distance between us and the males of our families had grown to an insurmountable gulf.

Not that we didn't love our brothers and fathers, but we understood their place as our superiors, as untouchable gods who were not supposed to step down and mingle with us, the common folk. Like Sun Kings, they expected our lives and desires to revolve around them, their desires and schedules. I was so young, still years from adolescence, when reality slapped me in the face—when I was put in my place, second to all males, and expected to grow up and act as an adult overnight.

Now when we went to Aqaba, we were part of the anonymous huddle of covered women no longer allowed to enjoy the magic of the sea. For even on the beaches Islam's conservative clothing shrouded us all. It is mainly men and small children who are allowed to enjoy the beaches and water sports. Women would never dare be seen in a swimsuit. They sit on the shore, fully clothed, and tend to the needs of their men and their children. They are allowed, though, to enter the water and try to swim as long as they wear their *shar'ia* attire. Sad and ludicrous—but too familiar—is the sight of a woman struggling to stay afloat while trying to beat her voluminous black dress back into the waves, as it billows up on the surface. It is an act of the frustrated futility that now seems an apt metaphor for the lives of Jordanian women.

So while our love for the sea never diminished, our interest in Aqaba did. By adolescence, I was still allowed to wear a swimsuit, but was forced to wear baggy shorts to my knees and a big T-shirt. Dalia, on the other hand, had to remain in full *shar'ia* attire. And in the end, both of us were forced to leave our love of swimming behind. Our families still made their annual visits to these places, and though Dalia and I still obediently went, we spent most of our time catering to our fathers and brothers rather than enjoying the place.

❧✦☙

Our families planned to leave for Aqaba mid-May, for the lure of water in a desert nation is powerful, especially in April and May, when the perfect weather improves Jordanians' mood; it makes them smile and sends them south from Amman in droves to reclaim the areas of the country usually filled with tourists. Joined by Arabs from the entire Middle East—Saudi Arabians, Syrians, Lebanese—they flock to places like Aqaba, the hot springs of Hammamat Ma'in, and the Dead Sea, despite water so salty that it cannot sustain any plant or animal life.

The Dead Sea, the closest of these spots to Amman, is the first to become congested. It's the lowest point on earth (409 meters below sea level) and is part of the border between Jordan and Israel. Locally, it is known as Al-Bahr Al-Mayit or Buhr Lut (Sea of Lot), an apt name since the water's incredibly high salt content (30 percent) is seven times higher than that of other oceans. The waters, with their high levels of various minerals, are supposed to be wonderful for your health, skin, and stress levels.

So Arabs flow down to the banks of the Dead Sea, looking like a tribe of seals, covered from head to toe in Dead Sea mud, enduring it for the cures it promises for a host of illnesses—arthritis, bronchial infections, allergies. Over the years the Jordanian government has tried to transform the area into a resort/spa by allowing hotels to build up along its shores. But now, the small area of shoreline left untouched and available to the public quickly becomes overcrowded. After the mud therapy and hours of floating like corks in the buoyant sea, most people head to the fresh waters of Hammamat Ma'in to rinse off caked layers of salt in its thermal springs.

Hammamat Ma'in is the most famous of Jordan's sixty thermal springs, all of them famous for their curative value and rumored to have been visited by Herod the Great and Cleopatra. The crowds soak in water that stays at a hot 113 degrees Fahrenheit (45 Celsius), soaking up more minerals. After spending a few days at the hot springs, the crowds then continue down the Desert Highway, or Dead Sea Highway, to Aqaba, which tourists love for archaeological sites dating from before Christ. But that is not what draws Arabs; it is the refreshing escape from the hot, rose-colored desert that fills the landscape south of Amman. At the very southern tip of our landlocked country, Aqaba is Jordan's only outlet to the Gulf of Aqaba and the seas beyond, its only real seaside resort. For us, as children, it was the door to an exotic world we could only imagine.

But this year, nothing could lure us from Amman. We had to try to find a way to avoid going. We realized that it would be both tricky and difficult to persuade our families to let us stay behind, to leave us alone, unguarded, for at least a week. We had to assure them that we were trustworthy enough. Since crimes such as theft are very rare in Amman, our fathers would mostly be concerned about whether we would continue to obey their rules in their absence. We hoped to use our computer classes as our excuse for staying home.

It was agreed. We had permission to stay behind. But not completely unchaperoned. My father arranged for my aunt and her husband, who lived less than ten minutes away, to keep an eye on us, and, amazingly, Dalia's father, Mahmood, agreed too. This was the first time that we'd be alone together, without our fathers and brothers lurking around every corner. We were a bit nervous, but mostly thrilled. Our fathers agreed that it would be easier for my aunt to check on us if we stayed in one house during the week, which pleased us even more.

If only they'd stay away for two weeks. But for at least a week, we'd be roommates and real sisters. That so overjoyed us that we were almost tempted to call off any dates with Michael and just enjoy the time together. But, of course, we didn't. Maneuvering around my aunt would not be a problem since she had responsibilities at home. All we'd have to deal with were a few long-winded phone calls from her, and maybe, though highly unlikely, a brief visit. We decided to stay at my house because my neighbors were younger, busier, and not as nosy as Dalia's. Once the arrangements were made, our excitement mounted until at last the glorious day of our families' departure arrived.

Dalia's family left first. They dropped her off at my house at 7:30 that Friday morning. They were driving straight to Aqaba and planned to spend the entire week there. My family ate breakfast, packed their cars, and finally began their journey to the Dead Sea a few hours later. We said our good-byes, reassured them that all was under control, and waited until we were sure they'd gone too far to turn back. Then we blasted the radio and danced around the house in celebration. Once we tired ourselves dancing, I picked up the phone and called Jehan. For an instant we even thought of inviting her and Michael over, almost forgetting that we still had neighbors and so the freedom we felt only existed within my house. We made plans to meet every day that week. We'd already decided to close the salon, so our schedules were open. Jehan managed to get Michael on the phone, and I went up to my room to pick out our wardrobe for the week as Dalia talked to him.

An hour later, Dalia rushed into my room and flung herself on top of the piles of clothing on my bed.

"He's so sweet," she said.

"Yes, he is. What did you two talk about?"

"Oh everything, and nothing. Guess what?" she said as she sat up.

"What?" I shot back, anxious to hear what she had to say.

"Tonight he wants to take us to a restaurant that has a live band, dancing, and Greek food."

"Tonight? I don't know if it's such a good idea to meet him at night. We still have to go in and out of this house. What if someone tells my dad they saw us leaving at night? What if my aunt calls while we're gone? Why can't we go this afternoon?"

"Because they only have music and dancing at night. I really want to go."

"It sounds like fun, but it's too risky. I think we should stick to afternoons."

"Oh, come on, we can get away with this, you know we can. They're all gone. All we have to do is find a way to sneak in and out of the house without the neighbors seeing us. If your aunt calls while we're out, we'll say we were sleeping and didn't hear the phone."

"I guess we can do that. But since it's your idea, smart girl, you figure out a way to sneak in and out. Jehan's coming, isn't she?"

"I don't think so. We'll be out late and I don't think her father will let her stay out that late, even with Michael."

"Well, then, why am I going? Why don't the two of you go alone? I think it would be more romantic. You could put on some rings and my cross, then you'll look like a married Christian couple."

"But Norma, I want you to see it too. I want you to come."

"You can tell me everything when you get back. And it'll look better to the neighbors if I stay here, making noise and burning lights. You can sneak in and out through the back."

"He's going to meet us on the next corner, behind the pizza place. I thought we could just walk over there, it's not that far."

"Well, you figured wrong. You're going to walk over there by yourself. You can bring me some Greek food to make up for leaving me behind. Besides, you and Michael need to spend some time alone."

After a year of dates it would be her first time alone with him. I could see she was nervous. But it was settled. "Now, let's pick out the perfect outfit. You have to look like a married woman, remember."

"Wait, what time is it? I have to run to the mosque." I knew this was not piousness, but attention to detail—the sheikh might tell her father she wasn't there.

"I completely forgot. You'd better get going; it's almost time for services. I wish you could just miss it."

She jumped up and began changing her clothes.

"I can't. My dad specifically reminded me to go this morning when he dropped me off. I'm sure he'll quiz me on it when he gets back." She started buttoning her *shar'ia* dress over her other clothing and adjusted her head veil. "I can't believe I almost forgot."

She kissed me and ran out of the house, leaving me circled by mountains of clothes. I picked out a few outfits for her date, then rummaged through the overfilled shelves and storage compartments in the refrigerator looking for leftovers from yesterday's *mulukiyyeh* (a thick spinach stew with chicken pieces served over a bed of rice, and topped with lemon)—one of our favorite dishes. As I cooked up some rice, waiting for Dalia, I noticed that the kitchen had been well-stocked by my father before he left, so we wouldn't have to leave the house to go shopping. His attention to detail was as good as ours, and that scared me a little.

When Dalia returned, she burst out laughing when she found me sitting in my father's recliner in the living room, smoking and drinking coffee. Dalia plopped down on the couch and reached for my coffee and a cigarette—her first ever in my living room. How delicious these small, forbidden pleasures.

"Well, Miss Dalia, I've arranged some outfits upstairs for your romantic evening with Michael. But first, you're joining me for lunch on the terrace. I've taken the liberty of preparing rice, and warming up the *mulukiyyeh*," I said in the formal voice of the maître d's we'd been hearing.

Suddenly Dalia looked deflated. She was apprehensive about meeting Michael alone. "I don't know how to act, or what to say or do."

"Oh, come on, Dalia, you know how to act. I think you're nervous because you really like him, and you know this is becoming serious. It may seem more serious to you because Jehan and I won't be there."

"Maybe that's part of it," she said.

"What did you just say? I can't believe it, you're actually agreeing with me?"

"I only said maybe, you don't need to make such a big deal over it. Anyway, I'm starved; let's go eat."

After how many thousands of lunches we had together, this was a new experience. We savored our freedom as we ate. We felt even more liberated than during our underground afternoons with Michael and Jehan. Today, we weren't worried about being caught. We took our time, relishing each morsel, treasuring every second, getting a dose of independence with every bite.

After lunch, we ran upstairs to pick out the perfect outfit for Dalia's evening. After hours of playing dress-up, we decided on a long, cotton summer dress painted with wildflowers and crimson roses that made her look magical. I could never envy her beauty, only admire it, because she made everyone around her feel beautiful. We decided that if she was going to look like a young Christian woman, she had to put on some makeup. But it couldn't cover her apprehension. Time flew as we chatted about the approaching evening and, before we knew it, it was time for her to go. We tiptoed out the back door and through the yard, almost certain that we weren't seen, and ran to our meeting point. I waited until Michael arrived, wanting to see his reaction when he saw Dalia. He pulled the car up to the curb, got out, and walked around to the passenger side to let her in. His eyes said it all. He was so delighted with how she looked, and was so clearly in love. I went home, confident that Dalia was in loving hands.

Dalia sauntered in around 11:30, with a look of contentment and joy that I'd never seen before. I immediately decided that she should see Michael alone for the rest of the week. After tonight I was certain that it wouldn't be difficult to convince Dalia of my plan.

We spent most of the night talking about her evening, and nibbling the Greek food she'd brought back. For the first time, Dalia told me that she was in love with Michael. She actually used the word. It terrified, as well as thrilled, me. I'd spent months trying to get her to say it, and thought it would bring me pure joy. But now, the reality, the implications, of what it meant hit home—the vast weight and power of thousands of years of cultural forces that would be mobilized against it. We'd been playing girlish games until now, caught up in the intrigue and the testing of our ability

to outwit our jailers. Tonight, we'd been giggling adolescents playing dress-up. Cinderella at the ball. I'd played the game, conspired,
spurred it on to make her happy—and to share some vicarious
excitement. I could hardly bear to ask myself: Has this all been a
terrible mistake? What pain and danger was I helping to bring
down on Dalia? And on myself?

But I wasn't sure we could stop it. Or that we wanted to.

THIRTEEN

The next few weeks and months raced by as Dalia and I continued to live our double lives. By the end of the summer we'd been to virtually every chic restaurant in Amman, or at least every one we were confident that none of our family members went to. Now we decided it was time to venture past the borders of the city. We wanted to go for a picnic together and started looking for a place that was comfortable, private, and scenic. It was August and Jordan was like an inferno, so anywhere we picked had to shade us from the scorching midday sun. But where?

Jordan has neither wide areas of lush greenery nor much wildlife. The country's dominant physical fact is the fertile valley of the Jordan River. Forming part of the Great Rift Valley of Africa, it rises just over the Lebanese border and continues along the entire length of Jordan from the Syrian border in the north to Aqaba and the Red Sea in the south. Fed by the Sea of Galilee (Lake Tiberias), the Yarmouk River, and the valley streams of the high plateaus to the east and west, the Jordan now lays stagnant, and the surrounding fertile areas are in danger. Jordan's biggest natural problem is the eternal one of deserts, lack of water, now worsened by its growing population, rising living standards in the cities, heavy exploitation for agriculture and, of course, waste. Jordan has lost millions of fertile hectares to desertification over the centuries and has lost with them a stable environment for wildlife, birds, or flora. Our candidate for the picnic was one of the six protected nature reserves maintained by Jordan's major environmental agency, the Royal Society for the Conservation of Nature.

We decided that one of the Society's two nature preserves nearest Amman would be perfect for our picnic. My first choice was Zai National Park, a small, dense pine forest, closest of the two to Amman, but Dalia and Jehan had their hearts set on Dibeen National Park, one of the last pine forests in Jordan for nature lovers and home to the endangered Persian squirrel. It also has great views and restaurants. So Dibeen it would be.

It was easy enough to come up with the plan, but it was much more complicated to put it in place. Our resourcefulness now knew no bounds. Jehan asked a friend from school to pose as a bride who wanted Dalia and me to style her wedding party, with a special request. Would we give her an in-home demonstration and consultation prior to her wedding day? Our job was to make sure that Mohammed believed the farce, and dropped us off at her house for four hours. We thought it would be easy enough to convince Mohammed. But we worried about involving a fifth person in our conspiracy, Jehan's friend. We called Jehan every day to make sure she'd taken care of all the details. Each time, she told us the same thing, "Calm down, don't worry. I've taken care of it, it's all set."

❦

On the afternoon of our picnic, we parked ourselves in Mohammed's pickup, hugging workbags packed with snacks and food. We'd made sure that Mohammed had other plans and so would not want to sit around and wait for us. But what would we find when we got to Jehan's friend's house? We were worried. We prayed that she would open the door if Mohammed decided to walk us up to the entrance, as he usually did. We didn't want to think about what would happen if her parents answered the door and we had to tell them, in front of Mohammed, that we were there for a wedding consultation with their daughter—who was not even engaged.

As Mohammed parked the car in front of a big, new multiunit building, Dalia and I nervously looked at one another as we got out of the pickup and Mohammed followed us to the door of the unit on the first floor. However, a young woman answered the door and escorted us into her home, as Mohammed left. We embraced Jehan, waiting inside, and celebrated the success of our plan so far.

"Sit down, relax, and have some tea. Michael should be here in about twenty minutes or so. This is Hanan, my best friend from school. Don't worry about anything, her mother passed away two years ago and her dad's at work, so we're all alone," Jehan said.

We sat in Hanan's drawing room, drank some mint tea, ate pastries, and talked while we waited for Michael. Soon, he came in with great excitement.

"Is everyone ready to go? Dalia, I have a surprise for you," he said, teasing as he led the parade to the car.

Dalia sat decorously in the backseat, with Jehan and me.

Suddenly the car was vibrating with the sound of Amir Diab's "Habbibi" song, Dalia's favorite.

"Oh my God, you got it. I can't believe you got it. Thank you!" she yelled.

"I found it at the Music Box in Fuheis," he replied.

Amir Diab's album had soared to the top of the charts shortly after its release. Everyone had raced out to buy a copy in the first few weeks, and now it was completely sold out. Dalia had been trying to get her hands on a copy for a while.

"How did you remember that I liked this song? I only told you it was my favorite once," she said.

"I remember everything you tell me," he replied.

I was impressed.

We arrived at Dibeen National Park, and chatted and giggled as we hiked through the pine forest, springing along the trails on a spongy carpet of pine needles, looking for the ideal picnic spot. We saw no one else on the trails. The park was ours.

We chose to sit in a small clearing that had an enchanted mix of shade and sunbeams, circled by an aromatic ring of pine trees. We spread our blankets on the ground and sat down, losing ourselves in conversation and feasting for the next few hours. At three, reluctantly, we left the park and went back to Hanan's house, and waited for Mohammed to pick us up.

Growing bolder, we planned the next picnic at Zai National Park, where Dalia and Michael would go by themselves. It took Jehan weeks to arrange.

❧✦❧

But Dalia's face when I saw her the next day after their picnic was worth it. We sat in the break room and she told me that, for the first time since meeting Michael, she had kissed him.

"Oh, Norma, I can't even begin to tell you how it felt. It was so incredible; I've never felt anything like that before. I felt as if a spark of electricity was shooting through every inch of my body. It was just . . . magic," she said.

She had been afraid. "But it wasn't awkward. It felt so natural. I really wanted to kiss him. I know that maybe I shouldn't have, since he's not my husband, but Norma, I love him, so totally and completely. It embarrasses me to say this, but he's the husband of my heart and mind, and that's what counts."

"You know, Dalia, we need to figure out exactly what you and Michael are going to do about this. It sounds like it's getting pretty serious. Have you two talked about it?"

"Well, of course we have. He's told me that he loves me and I've told him that I love him. If it weren't for our religious differences, he'd ask my father for permission to marry me right now. But Michael could never convert to Islam; it would destroy his family, and a thousand laws would come down on my head if I tried to convert to Catholicism. So we're stuck."

"But if you two lived in a different country, a non-Muslim country, you could be married."

"Sure we could. But we're living in Jordan, so we're stuck."

"You're stuck if you stay here, but maybe you could go somewhere else. Michael went to school in London and he's traveled a lot; maybe he can find a way to get you out."

"Norma, do you realize what you're saying? If he *could* do something like that, and I went through with it, then you and I might never see each other again."

"Dalia, I know exactly what I'm saying. But *think* about it . . . you'd be free to marry the man you love. You could live the way you want, and have children, and raise them the way you want to. You can have daughters who would have rights, more rights than women here ever dream of having."

"I'd love to spend the rest of my life with him and I want to have his children, but I don't want to be without you."

"Who knows what tomorrow holds, right? For all you know, I might leave Jordan one day. But you can't think of me. I'll always love you, and you can't run away from your destiny for my sake. If you two love each other the way I know you do, and you can find a way to be together, then you should go."

"I don't see why we can't all go together."

"We'll talk to Michael and see what he can do, if anything. If it's possible for both of us to escape, then I'll come too. But even if I can't get out, you have to go. It's where you belong."

"Norma, if you come that's one thing, but I don't know if I could leave without you."

"Dalia, even if I don't come now, we'll find ways to stay in touch. Eventually you'll probably find some way for me to join you. But right now, this is about you and Michael, not about you and me."

Tears sprang to her eyes. "I do love him and I know he feels the same way. I'll talk to him and see if he can find a way to get us out of here. He will, I know he will."

For days she was lost in her own romantic universe. She reveled in her emotions, and thought only about the man she loved. I believed that if paradise could exist on earth, she'd found it. She was in a world I couldn't share, but could only hope to experience one day.

FOURTEEN

Who knew that a fistful of pine needles would plant the first seeds of serious doubt in our minds that our conspiracy would do anything but succeed? We'd been nervous at first, but with every new success our confidence had grown. And when the doubt came, it would shock us out of the dream world Dalia inhabited, and the unsettling new emotions I'd struggled with since I'd heard the news that she and Michael would move away and be married. It had never occurred to me, ever, that Dalia's relationship with Michael could cause us to be separated forever. On one hand, I was ecstatic for her, but I also envied her. I tried to persuade myself that it wasn't Dalia herself who I envied, but what she had discovered. I'd always loved Dalia as if she were my sister, and I truly believed that nothing could or would ever change that. Now I realized that my jealousy was driven both by a need to understand what she felt and a feeling that I didn't want to share her with Michael.

I didn't doubt Michael's affection for her or his integrity. I knew that if I lost her to Michael, she'd be in safe hands. But that didn't make me feel much better, and it didn't help me forget the fact that I might never see her again. More than anything, I truly did want her to be happy, and I knew that without Michael she wouldn't be and that they needed to leave Jordan in order to be together. As she blissfully sailed through the days and weeks that followed, swept by the power of these new emotions, I worked to hide mine. I was worried that if she knew what I was feeling, she'd never agree to go away, and I didn't want to stand in her way.

Either I was doing an excellent job or Dalia was so enveloped in her own thoughts that she never sensed my conflict. One Thursday, a few weeks after Dalia's declaration of love, we were planning to get together to bake sweets and talk as usual. Our *sihra* was to be at Dalia's house, and I had permission to go directly there after closing the salon. We'd decided to make *kunafay* because it was her brother Nasar's favorite dessert, and he and his wife were coming for a visit. We didn't particularly enjoy Nasar's company, but we wanted to encourage him to visit more often for his wife, Diane's, sake, since he usually kept her locked up at home.

Dalia had spent that whole week talking to Michael about leaving Jordan and, as I arrived, I could tell that she had something urgent to report. As we prepared the desserts in her kitchen, she was clearly bursting to talk. But she insisted that we finish baking so that she could spill it out later, uninterrupted, in her room. Michael must have found a way to get them out of Jordan, I guessed. I didn't want to start sobbing and dissuade her from leaving when she told me, but I hadn't yet found a way to stay strong. I prayed that the baking would drag on. But the *kunafay* was ready in record time.

Then Nasar and Diane walked in. I thanked God for their arrival, as it postponed our conversation a little longer. We could never have left them and locked ourselves in Dalia's room, or expect Dalia's mother to serve them alone. So Dalia began brewing the coffee as I poured the syrup over the *kunafay*.

The living room was filled with Dalia's family, all watching TV. All four of her brothers, her mother, her father, and Diane seemed mesmerized by a Spanish series that had been translated into Arabic. Jordanian television has only four channels, and all of them go off the air by midnight. Most don't broadcast movies, and so any program that was not news or a Muslim religious show usually had a captive following. As we served the coffee and desserts and sat down on the love seat next to Diane, everyone kept their eyes on the television while shoveling bite-sized pieces of *kunafay* into their mouths. The first commercial break ended the silence, soon replaced by banter about our cooking, with Mohammed joking that my *kunafay* had almost put him in the emergency room.

Everyone giggled as Mohammed and I went through our regular Thursday night routine. Since we were not allowed to banter with any man outside of our families, we enjoyed this weekly sparring, permitted only by our friendship, which had turned Dalia's family into an extension of my own and vice versa.

"Well, their cooking has definitely improved since they decided to practice every Thursday, although they've made some strange things. If I didn't know any better, I'd swear it was a conspiracy to hospitalize us all," Mohammed joked.

The word "conspiracy" shook me alert. My shoulders stiffened.

"You, maybe, but what could we possibly have against everyone else?" I teased back, nervous that there was an edge to his comment.

"Oh, I'm sure if I took the time to think about it, I could come up with some reason you two would want to hurt me, reasons that would probably even be believable," he shot back. I froze. This didn't feel like innocent teasing anymore.

Dalia's father chimed in before I had to respond.

"*Yaba*, go make some tea," he said. And with that, Dalia and I collected the plates and went into the kitchen.

"How long do you think they're going to stay?" I whispered to Dalia.

She carried the tea tray out to the living room. Everyone was again glued to the Spanish soap opera. Mohammed and Nasar quickly stood to leave.

"Don't you want tea?" I asked.

"We're going to go wash the pickup," Mohammed said as they left.

"Girls, please make some lemonade and take it out to Nasar and Mohammed," Dalia's mother asked at the next commercial. They were busy cleaning the pickup in the driveway, with both their heads buried inside the truck, scrubbing the upholstery and chatting. As we got nearer, we heard bits of their conversation.

"There are only two places in Amman that have this," Nasar was saying.

"One of your friends probably left it. You're always lugging them around town."

As we held the glasses out toward them, Mohammed walked around the car to take his lemonade. As he stepped up he threw a small fistful of pine needles to the ground, at my feet, and I felt another charge of fear. Dalia had noticed them, too. The park. Our picnic. Needles must have clung to our blankets—or shoes, workbags. Oh, God, oh, God. But we didn't react. We gave them their drinks and hurried back into the kitchen.

"Oh my God, Norma. Did you see that?" she said in a panic.

"Yes. But did you hear what Nasar was saying, that one of Mohammed's friends probably left them? I'm sure he believed that, so don't worry," I said, trying to calm myself as well.

"Norma, what do you mean don't worry? Oh my God, this is horrible, horrible."

"It's not good, but it's not that horrible either. Mohammed is always driving his friends around, he'll probably just forget about it."

We sat nervously for the next hour until Nasar and Diane left, waiting for Mohammed to bring up the pine needles. He didn't. He must have assumed that the pine needles had been left by one of his friends.

Later, in Dalia's room, we laughed about the incident and moved on to more important things: Michael.

"He said that he thinks he can probably get us visas for London or Greece. He has friends in both those countries who will put us up until we get settled," she announced.

"That's wonderful. Then you can get married. You know how much I'll miss you, but you have to do this," I said, trying to be positive.

"No, you don't understand. He's going to try to get the visas for all three of us."

"What? Are you sure? Did he say that? Oh my God, I can come with you? Dalia, no, that would be too much. What would his friends say? I can understand the two of you staying with them, but me too?"

"He's talked to his friends and they're fine with it. You have to come. I don't want to go without you. Please say you'll come. We'll all be free. We have some money saved, and so does he, so we'll be fine."

"Dalia, you make it sound so simple. You're talking about moving to a foreign country, with a new language, new customs, and new people. Finding new jobs."

"Come on, Norma, nothing you want badly enough is ever simple, you know that. We can do this, you'll see." I was caught up in her optimism. Suddenly I was laughing as it sank in. Freedom!

"I can't think of anything I'd like better than being homeless and penniless with you and Michael in a foreign country. Okay, let's do it!"

"You mean it?"

"Yes!" I hugged her shoulders and looked into the eyes of my best friend. "You think I'd let you go alone? I was so worried that you'd be leaving and that I'd never see you again. Now, we can leave together! This is the best news of my whole life."

We pushed the pine needles to the back of our minds, where they couldn't dilute the euphoric sense of hope we were feeling as we talked through the details. We were so close to Greece—or London—that I could almost see the tickets and visas in our hands. By the time my father arrived to pick me up, we were confident that it was all going to work, and appeared completely calm, though inside I was vibrating with possibilities.

FIFTEEN

Toward the end of September, Dalia went to Zai National Park with Michael for one more picnic. There she told him that I'd agreed to join them and they shared another kiss, which made her ecstatic for days. When she got back, we began to figure out what we had to do in order to leave with Michael, and found that it was more difficult than we'd originally thought. There were hundreds of specifics to consider, and logistical bits and pieces we hadn't expected. We spent three sleepless nights thinking up plans and filled our days discussing our ideas. It was further complicated by the onset of Ramadan. While Ramadan is not a public holiday, most businesses are either closed or have shorter hours during the month-long holiday. It's also against the law for any citizen, whether Muslim or not, to eat, smoke, or drink in public during the day. Since Dalia had to abide by these rules, I did the same to make it easier for her.

The problems we were facing, however, had little to do with the rules of Ramadan; they were caused by the erratic hours most of the government offices kept during this month. Michael had lots of contacts in the embassies and government offices we had to go to in order to get our visas. We decided to gather all our paperwork and have him try to process the papers through his friends, hoping he could get them without either of us being there. This was when we came across our biggest stumbling block. It was something so obvious that we should have thought about it the moment we started talking about leaving Jordan. Dalia and I needed passports. Since we'd never been outside Jordan, we didn't have them. Before Michael could get us visas, we had to have passports. Before we could buy airplane tickets, we had to have passports. Passports became our new nightmare. And, it can be hard to get a passport in Jordan if you don't want your family to know about it. Since we were women, we had to produce three pieces of paper to get one issued: a birth certificate, a picture identification card, and our family book. In Jordan, the male head of a family, in our cases our fathers, is issued a family book. While it looks a bit like a passport, it's actually a family record that details genealogy and gives reference to the family book in which a person was previously listed. Our fathers' family books listed our mothers, our siblings, and us. Using this system, the government can keep a record of all families, and they also ensure that no woman can travel without her parents' consent. Men only need the first two, the birth certificate and ID; they don't need to furnish a family book. We had our birth certificates and identification cards; the problem was the family book. We realized that we would have to find a way to get them without our fathers' knowledge and pray that the passport office wouldn't call our parents when we appeared. In the meantime, Michael searched for some way to create passports without using our family books.

It was during this time that Dalia's behavior began to change. Over several days, her excitement vanished, replaced by fear and anxiety. At first I thought it was just nerves, though she insisted it

126

wasn't. Since the pine needles, she'd been on alert, watching Mohammed for signs. Now she was sure that we'd been discovered. I was so focused on trying to arrange our escape that I hadn't paid much attention to Dalia's growing suspicions.

"Norma, I'm positive Mohammed knows something. He hasn't been himself lately, not toward me, at least. I'm really anxious," she said.

"Dalia, that's impossible. You're just worried that we won't be able to pull this off and it's getting to you," I replied.

"Of course I'm worried about pulling this off, but that's not what I'm talking about. Mohammed is acting very different; he even looks at me differently."

I went over everything we had planned since she'd met Michael in an attempt to convince her that no one suspected anything, but the more I talked, the more nervous she became. She was just feeling emotionally vulnerable since her relationship with Michael was now becoming more serious, I tried to tell myself. Maybe she was having second thoughts, or feeling guilty because she'd kissed him, and that was making her paranoid.

But the more I tried to persuade her that her fears were unfounded, the more she insisted that I was wrong. We stopped planning our escape in order to try to calm her down, but nothing seemed to work. Within a few days, she had turned, quite literally, into a nervous wreck. She wasn't sleeping or eating properly—I had never seen her like this. I searched for ways to ease her anxiety, but came up empty-handed. She was obsessed with the pine needles Mohammed had found in his truck, and insisted that he'd suspected something ever since, although he'd never said a word to either of us. I tried to believe her, but couldn't get past the idea that if he suspected us he'd have said something. His behavior toward us in the salon had not changed, but I knew that this didn't entirely disprove Dalia's theory, since Mohammed was unlikely to change his public behavior regardless of what he believed in private. I continued to believe that Dalia's transformation was due to nerves over the seriousness of what we were about to do. Dalia remained convinced that her relationship with Michael had been discovered.

SIXTEEN

Dalia's mood worsened as the days went by, aggravated by lack of sleep. In all the years I'd known her, she'd always been able to compose herself, betraying none of the emotional turmoil she was experiencing, but this time it was clear that she was losing control. I grew even more worried when she refused to come to my home one Sunday afternoon, and my anxiety peaked the following day as we walked to the salon.

"Dalia, you look really tired. Have you slept at all?" I asked.

"No, I can't sleep. Something is really wrong at home, Norma. I'm so worried that I can't think straight anymore," she replied.

"I really think you're worrying about nothing. I don't know what I need to do to convince you that you're wrong about this," I said as I unlocked the door to the salon and went in. She followed me into the break room and, as I began brewing coffee, she flung herself on the couch and emitted an exasperated sigh.

"Norma, I'm not wrong. Do you know what Mohammed did yesterday?" she said, sitting up. "When I was about to walk to your house, he insisted on taking me. He wouldn't let me out of the house alone. Also, he kept asking me about this week's appointments at the salon. He wanted to know the exact times of the appointments and which clients were scheduled to come in. That's why I didn't come over."

"Dalia, he's probably trying to schedule something with his friends and wants to find a way to fit it in. I think you're reading way too much into this," I said as I poured the coffee and joined her on the couch.

She held a cigarette with shaky fingers, brought it up to her lips, and inhaled as though it would give her the ability to go on.

"No, you're wrong. He's never asked for such specific information before. And I've been walking to your house on Sundays for how many years?" she said tensely, as she drew in more smoke. "Now he insists that he has to drive me. Why? I know why and he knows, that's why."

It was as if she needed me to confirm her suspicions, even though I believed that would have pushed her over the edge. "Relax. Calm down. I'm sure there's some other reason. He was probably going out and planned to pass my house, so he decided to drop you off. You've been so worried that you're seeing everything differently. You really need to relax. Why don't you stay back here and try to get some rest today? Sleep a little; I'll take your appointments or reschedule them for you."

"No, I can't. I have to find a way to discover what he knows. I have to know or I'll go nuts. I haven't been able to think of anything else for days. We have to figure out a way," she said as she lit her second cigarette.

"Dalia, please, stay back here today and get some rest. Then we'll figure out a way to get some answers. I promise." I left the break room to set up the salon for our first appointment. All morning, I thought about Dalia in the break room. Her mood had changed so dramatically in just a few short days. There had to be a way to bring her happiness back.

Every so often Dalia would wander out of the break room. She would circle the salon as if she were disoriented and had never seen the salon before. Each time she appeared, I took her by the arm and gently led her back to the couch, all the while praying that Mohammed wouldn't show up and see her like this. If he did, then he would definitely start asking questions, which would push her over the edge.

I canceled most of our appointments that day, hoping to have more time to talk her out of this paranoid depression. I felt like I could see her being swept by her fears into a sea of suffering, as I stood powerless on the shore. With each day, her phobia was drawing her further and further out of my reach. She was so enveloped in her terror that I couldn't get through to her. She had locked me out. For the first time in over twenty years, I felt distanced from her, and it really scared me.

I did what I could to comfort her until Mohammed showed up to close the salon. I'd repeatedly begged her to stay quiet on the way home, so Mohammed wouldn't notice her nervousness. I kept assuring her that we would find out if he knew anything, and realized that in order to save her sanity I would have to find a way to convince her that he didn't.

But it did occur to me—what if she was right? She knew Mohammed; they shared the same house. She'd never in her life shown anything like this disabling paranoia. But then she had never before put her life on the line for a forbidden romance. I didn't dare tell her, but a shadow of her fear was beginning to fall over me, too.

SEVENTEEN

After months of feeling trapped in an airless oven with daily temperatures well above 100 degrees Fahrenheit, I woke up in the predawn hours of that Tuesday to the eerie echo of the muezzins' call to the faithful to pray. *"La illaha illa Allah Mohammed rasul Allah"* was being broadcast from the loudspeakers of the many mosques throughout Amman and its surrounding suburbs.

I'd spent most of the night wrestling with both my thoughts and the sheets, and so I welcomed the cool winds of early morning. It was a sure sign that the heat wave was finally loosening its grip on the city. The short, cool bursts of air blowing in through my partially opened bedroom window, along with the memory of my phone conversation with Dalia the previous night, made me shiver.

As I thought about the hours and months we'd spent planning and scheming in order to make Dalia's relationship with Michael a reality, a sudden panic rose from deep inside me, trapping my breath in my throat. Maybe her suspicions weren't paranoid or based on guilt. Maybe the only reason I didn't want to acknowledge her fears was that I knew how grave the consequences would be if her family found out. Suddenly I was desperate to talk to her.

Our phone conversation the previous night had taken on a whole new dimension. I started analyzing every phrase and struggled to recall the tone of her voice.

"Hello, Norma. Can you talk for a minute?" she asked.

"Sure, what's wrong? You sound upset."

"I'm worried, Norma. I'm really worried. Mohammed is getting weirder by the minute and now my dad is acting strange, too."

"What do you mean?"

"Well, he came into my room a while ago to make sure I was keeping the *Sala* and performing my nightly prayers. Then he told me that I wouldn't have to make breakfast in the morning."

"That's strange, but I'm sure there's some explanation."

"I think they both know something. My father hasn't asked me if I was keeping the *Sala* since I was sixteen. And what about Mohammed? He's been avoiding me for two days. When we bump into each other, he gives me a really mean look. What's all that about? I mean we're not really that close, but he's never treated me like this before."

"Come on, Dalia, relax. No one knows anything. Calm down and go to bed. You're just paranoid and you haven't slept for a week. I'm sure you're reading too much into all of this. Maybe Mohammed is upset about something and is taking it out on you, and, who knows, maybe your dad just wanted to give you a break from your regular morning chores. I can tell that you're very tired; I'm sure they've noticed too."

"Norma, please. I'm not paranoid or crazy. Something isn't right here, I feel it."

"Dalia, come on, just relax and get some rest. You'll see; it'll all look different in the morning. We'll talk about it some more tomorrow."

"Oh, Norma, I'm really scared. I can't sleep."

"Dalia, you have to sleep. You're worrying me and you're going to make yourself sick. I'm sure it's not what you think it is; there's no way they could know anything. Please, just try to relax."

"I hope you're right, Norma, but something just doesn't feel right. I can't wait until I can get out of here."

"*Yalla ya gazallae*, clear your head and go to bed, and I'll see you in the morning as usual."

"*In sha Allah ya hillweh*," she said and reluctantly hung up.

❧❧

As I went over the conversation, I jumped out of bed. I hastily dressed, neglecting all of my morning chores, telling my family that I didn't feel well, grabbed a light jacket, and sat on the veranda staring in the direction of Dalia's house. Suddenly I understood all of the anxiety and dread that Dalia had been desperately trying to communicate to me over the past two days. I kept looking at my watch, wishing I could will the next thirty minutes to pass. In a futile attempt to clear my mind, I tried to concentrate on the panorama of the city, and its transformation from a ghost town to a bustling metropolis.

Amman was born on seven *jebels* (hills), but today it spreads across nineteen. From my house near the highest point of Jebel Hussein, I had a clear view of most of the streets below and of the surrounding *jebels*. I took in the entire view of the endless, hilly landscape dotted with hundreds upon hundreds of square gray concrete buildings, separated only by roads and minarets that towered above the lifeless-looking dwellings. The sun had risen a few hours before and had already begun its struggle to break through the sandy haze that blanketed the city. There were a few cars headed toward the entrance ramp of Kings Highway, trying to beat the morning traffic. I could see housewives on their roofs, hanging laundry and shaking out area rugs. Soon schoolchildren would fill the streets, their loud banter and laughter destroying what was left of the morning quiet.

I looked at my watch and was filled with anxiety. She should have been here by now, I thought, especially since she's not making breakfast today. I began to wonder what could be keeping her. After our last conversation, I assumed that she'd have been in a hurry to leave the house and eager to talk. I became increasingly alarmed.

I began to pace the length of the terrace, stopping only to stare down Khalid bin al-walid Road. Around 8:45, I began to think that every figure on the street, male or female, was Dalia. By 8:55, I was frantic and every second that passed felt like an eternity. I ran through the house and pounced on the phone as if it were my lifeline. I struggled to dial her number and, after two wrong attempts, I was able to steady my index finger long enough to dial correctly. The phone rang six times, with what felt like days dragging between each ring. Maybe no one is home and she is on her way here . . . impossible . . . where would her mother be? Maybe the whole family went somewhere together? She'd have called to let me know that she wasn't coming. Maybe she overslept and no one heard the phone? Unlikely, since she never misses her morning prayers. Maybe she's sick? After all, she hasn't eaten or slept all week. And, again I resolved that she would have called. It wasn't like Dalia to forget to call. Any reasonable explanation I thought of dissolved when I realized that she would have called me to explain why she was late.

By nine, I was a walking time bomb and in no mood to obey any rules. I scrambled past my parents to the door, ignoring my father's inquiries and demands to stop. On any other day I would never have dared to do such a thing. I knew better than to leave the house without receiving my father's approval first. It had taken months of constant begging to get his permission to walk the few blocks to the salon with Dalia in the morning. Charging out of the house alone was a first for me. I think the only reason my father didn't get up and stop me was because he was so shocked that I would even consider such a thing that it rendered him immobile.

As I headed down the street in the direction of Dalia's house, the road seemed to double in length before my eyes. The remote sound of sirens filled the streets, and the closer I came to her house, the louder they seemed. I turned off Nablus Street onto Khalid bin al-walid Road and stopped when I saw an ambulance, its lights flashing, in front of Dalia's house. My legs began to tremble and I felt as if they'd give out. A sick terror shot through my body, and I knew that my heart had stopped. My worry about Dalia propelled me forward, while my fear struggled to pull me back. "Please, God, let her be okay," echoed in my head, and I tried to convince myself that the emergency vehicles were at her neighbor's house. As soon as I got to her house, the ambulance began to drive away, lights flashing and sirens blaring, telling me that it had someone inside.

Dalia's front door was open and most of her neighbors were surveying the scene from their balconies. I glanced around and saw that none of the neighbors were visibly distraught. They looked curious, not concerned, and I knew that the passenger in the ambulance must have come from Dalia's house. I rushed up the stairs to her front door, going up two at a time. I burst into the family room and found myself enveloped by a frightening stillness and a cloud of tension so thick that I could almost see it.

Her mother and four brothers were sitting there, all at a distance apart from one another. Her mother glanced up at me and I noticed that her eyes were swollen and red. She lowered her head, covered her face with her hands, and began to sway back and forth, obviously fighting back tears. She was the only one who showed any emotion other than anger, which flashed from the men. The four young men I'd known all my life didn't even bother to acknowledge my presence. Mohammed, who'd spent hours upon hours with us at the salon over the past six years, didn't even glance in my direction. For an instant, I decided that something must have happened to Mahmood, Dalia's father. One look at her mother told me that whatever had happened was serious. I was about to start asking questions when Mahmood appeared in the doorway. As soon as I saw him and before I could open my mouth, my legs collapsed and I fell to my knees. I knew now that Dalia was the passenger in the ambulance. I took a moment to gather my strength and absorb the shock. My mouth was so dry that I didn't think I could talk, even if I wanted to. My hands were trembling and I felt dizzy and light-headed, but I had to find out what had transpired and somehow forced the words out.

"What happened? Where is she?" I asked.

The only person who responded was her father. "Where is she? Where she belongs, that's where she is!" he said angrily.

"What do you mean? What happened?" I asked.

I waited for a moment and when he didn't reply, I asked again, "Where is she?"

"Don't worry, if I find out you knew, or helped her in any way, you'll be following her shortly," he snapped. The dehumanized way he looked at me and spoke his icy words told me exactly what he meant, but I had to press on. Had to know.

"Following her? Please tell me what happened! Tell me where they took her!" I pleaded.

"God's will is what happened! What did she think? That my home is a house of whoredom?" he yelled.

"What are you talking about?" I asked.

"About her and that Catholic man, that's what I'm talking about. How long did you two think you could hide it from me? How long has she been shaming me and dishonoring my good name?" he hollered.

"I don't know what you're talking about. You've made a mistake. Dalia never shamed you. She never would. Please tell me what you've done. Is she okay?" I asked.

"I've cleaned my house, that's what I've done. I've cut out the rotten part and brought honor back to my family name. From now on, no one is allowed to mention that name to me again. I never had a daughter! Understood?" he shouted as he glared, first at me and then at the rest of his family.

"Please, you've made a terrible mistake. She never shamed you; she will never shame you. Just tell me if she's okay. Please, let me see Dalia!" I begged.

"There is no Dalia here! Now leave and don't mention that name to me again."

It was as if he were speaking a different language, but the words kept repeating in my head. While I now understood that Dalia was dead, that he'd killed her, I couldn't accept it. I tried to be strong. I really did. I tried to detach myself from what was happening and pretend that I was just a spectator and not a participant, but I couldn't separate myself from the horrifying reality. Although I knew this had always been one of the risks, it had been an abstract threat to us, and the power of our successes had pushed it back.

We'd begun to feel invincible. I was not prepared to face the fact of it. I didn't know how to handle it. A storm of anger gathered inside and broke into a scream.

"NO! I won't leave! I want Dalia! Do you hear me? I said Dalia! She's your daughter! How can you deny that she exists? I won't leave here without Dalia!" I shouted hysterically as tears flooded my eyes and I began wailing. As how many centuries of grieving Arab women had before me.

Before I could control my sobbing, my parents arrived. I didn't see them come in, but I saw my father standing next to Dalia's, shaking his hand, and heard my mother repeatedly saying, *"Min isnaq ya siddi, min isnaq,"* begging his pardon for my behavior. I couldn't believe what was happening—that they did not instantly run to the side of a distraught daughter. I was furious. I stood up and ran between my father and Mahmood, pulling their hands apart.

"Don't shake his hand! He killed her! He's a murderer! His hands are stained with innocent blood!" I yelled.

My parents, as well as everyone else there, were taken aback. My mother grabbed me, pulled me to her, and instantly began apologizing and begging Mahmood's pardon.

"Please, sir, I beg your pardon, I'm so sorry for her behavior. She doesn't mean it. She's obviously in shock and doesn't realize the weight of her words. Excuse her, please," she kept repeating as she tried to pull me toward the door. My father remained where he was and I could hear Dalia's father saying to him, "I've cleaned my house and I advise you to make sure that your house is clean, too. I don't know if Norma was involved in any of this, but I've done my part and told you that she may be."

Before my father could respond, I wrestled free and ran back to Mahmood. I wanted to look him right in the eyes as I said what I needed to say.

"Dalia never shamed you, you shamed yourself. You've turned your home into a house of murder. The spilling of her innocent blood has stained your name, your hands, and your soul forever. I will not rest until her death is avenged. You'll pay for this senseless slaughter! You're a murderer and there's no honor in that!"

My mother ran toward me, all the while repeating her list of apologies. My father grabbed me by my arm, spun me around, and slapped me across the face. Then he pushed me into my mother's arms and ordered her to take me outside.

I fully understood the gravity of my words, and I meant every word I said. I knew that hundreds of women had been killed for lesser offenses. Honor killing has always been part of the Middle East, even more deeply rooted than the religions that seemed to rule us. Before the birth of Christianity and Islam, when Arabia was populated and ruled by nomadic tribes, a sheikh's power was determined by his honor. In the pages of both the Bible and the Koran, one can find stories of women being stoned and killed for threatening the integrity and honor of their male rulers. Middle Easterners, Shi'ite and Sunni Muslims, as well as the various Christian sects that dwell there today, still believe in the towering importance of a man's honor. Any action by a woman that can be seen as disrespectful toward men and the traditional way of life warrants an honor killing. Requires it! As a woman, I knew that I didn't have the right to speak to a man in this manner—that I was inviting my own death. But at that moment my mind was focused on one thing: avenging the death of my best friend.

ॐ

Once I was on the street, I began denying that any of this was real. It had to be a nightmare. I would soon wake up. I had to see Dalia; I had to go to her. I tried to think for a moment and realized that the ambulance must have taken her to Palestine Hospital on Queen Alia Street, since it was the closest. I begged my mother to let me go, but she would not. She held onto my arm with deadly force, while urging me to calm down. She kept saying, with a pleading whisper, "*You* could be killed if you don't control your mouth." I could see she was scared of what my father would do if she let me go, but I had no more patience. I refused to waste any more time begging and explaining. My father would have plenty of time to reprimand and punish me once I came home from the hospital. I knew he would, but right now I had to go. I tore my arm from my mother's grip and ran toward Al-Istiqlal Road to flag down a taxi.

The taxi came to an abrupt stop in the circular drive in front of Palestine Hospital and I bolted out the door, yelling back to the driver that he would have to wait and drive me home if he wanted to get paid. I grabbed the first nurse I could find and asked her where they took patients who were brought in by ambulance. I raced to the emergency room and gave the attendant Dalia's full name, but I could tell by the grim look on her face that I was too late. She called a doctor over to talk to me and I was told that Dalia had been dead when she'd arrived at the hospital. There was nothing anyone could do, he said; Dalia had been stabbed twelve times in the chest. The image of Mahmood now merged with that of a bloody knife, driven in again and again, going beyond honor to the most primitive brutality, and I thought I'd be sick. Had I known then that after the stabbing he had waited before calling the ambulance to make sure that she could not be saved, I think I would have killed him.

I begged the doctor to let me see her, and he finally agreed. He instructed the nurse to take me to the morgue.

When we got into the elevator to go to the basement of the old hospital, it took all of my strength to keep from losing control, but I couldn't stop the flow of tears down my cheeks. I found a strange comfort in the fact that Dalia had been brought to the hospital where we'd both been born. In some odd way it seemed as if her life had somehow come full circle. In a daze, I followed the nurse down a long, dimly lit hallway into a large back room. She reached for the light switch and I was temporarily blinded by the bright lights overhead, which gave off an eerie, amplified, humming sound that broke the surreal silence.

The morgue had four stainless steel tables. On three, bodies were draped with white sheets. She walked to the nearest table and gently pulled the blood-soaked sheet back, revealing only Dalia's face. I thought I was ready to see her, but nothing could have prepared me for what now lay in front of me. The nurse reached out and laid her hand on mine. I felt a sharp pain tear through my chest. All the feelings I'd controlled, so that I could be strong for us both against an enemy whose allies were every Arab man in Jordan, surfaced. I started sobbing so hard I couldn't breathe. Dalia lay in front of me and, if not for the dry splatter of blood that stained parts of her beautiful face, she appeared to be in a deep sleep. I bent down, kissed her cheek and then pressed my cheek to hers while my tears spilled onto her cold face. I whispered to her, promising that I would not allow her death to be in vain, and kissed her forehead as I told her that I would always love her. The whole morning had seemed to stretch out into an eternity and even stopped several times, but now the few moments I had with Dalia flew by. My time with her was over before it had begun, here in the morgue and in the lives we thought we'd share.

When the nurse saw that I had managed to calm down a bit,

she asked me to leave. I carried a clear image of Dalia's face with me, one I knew would haunt me for the rest of my days. Standing outside the hospital, I cursed the cool winds I had welcomed earlier that morning for bringing this devastation to my life. In just a few hours, my world had fallen apart. I felt as if I'd been thrown into the desert and left alone to die.

EIGHTEEN

As I stood in the center of Palestine Hospital's ring-shaped drive, I knew that the direction of my life had permanently altered. I'd spent years supporting Dalia's fantasy of democracy and freedom for women without saying a word, too timid to add my voice to hers. I could suddenly see my whole life as a cowardly lie. I'd conformed to traditions I didn't believe in, and hidden my hope for freedom behind a wall of silence and a smile. Losing Dalia in this way made vivid to me something I'd always known but had managed to ignore. I could no longer hide my true emotions and beliefs in the hope that my silent cries would be heard. In memory of Dalia, I vowed to transform my silence into audible screams for justice and equal rights.

My first barrier was my father and brothers, who were waiting at home. Even if I managed to survive—and I now knew that my life was in clear danger from the men in both families—I would have to climb a centuries-old mountain before I could hope for any change. Fueled by a lifetime of suppressed anger, sparked now by the rebellious emotions Dalia's murder had provoked, I felt filled with a quiet, determined fire as I prepared to go home and face whatever came.

My taxi driver appeared from behind a line of oncoming traffic and began honking. I dropped myself into the backseat, mumbled my address, slammed the door, shut my eyes tightly, and began to replay the last few days in my mind. Dalia knew something was wrong and I'd refused to believe her. She'd felt this coming and I'd tried to convince her that she was paranoid. During the last few days of her life, when she'd needed me the most, I hadn't been there as I should have been. I tried to imagine what she'd felt during those last few days and the pain of her last few hours. I saw her face and her uncomprehending eyes as her father raised the knife. I drove myself crazy thinking about what I might have done or said to have prevented this. Spontaneously, her face was there again. In a stroke—in twelve strokes—that knife has taken her life, her laugh. I would never see or hear them again.

The taxi jerked to a stop in front of my house. I opened my eyes and stumbled out, in a trance, telling the driver to come to the house and collect his fare from my father. The driver was apprehensive and began saying, *"Khaliha alla Allah ya binty,"*—the ride is free, from God. I insisted that he escort me, not only to get the fare but to confirm where I'd been for the past hour. We marched up to the front door and I rang the bell. My father opened the door. I could tell by the look on his face he was shocked to see me standing beside a man. I pushed past him without saying a word, leaving him and the taxi driver to work things out.

Inside, I was disoriented, didn't recognize my surroundings. My home suddenly felt very alien and I wandered around, desperately searching for comfort and privacy. I finally dragged myself to my room, closed the door, and collapsed onto my bed. I pulled my knees to my chest and lay in a fetal position. I tried to brace myself for the wave of emotions I knew would now take over. Tears flowed down my face, soaking my pillow, as I gave in and descended into even deeper despair.

Unexpectedly, my bedroom door flew open with startling force, smashing into the dresser and knocking over the knickknacks I'd collected over the years. I opened my eyes to find my father standing in the doorway, hands on his hips, and eyes burning with rage. I sat up slowly and waited for his attack to begin.

"I don't approve of what you did at Mahmood's house. It was very disrespectful, and I won't stand for my daughter to be known as disrespectful," he raged.

I wrapped my arms around my pillow and buried my head in it.

"I've talked to Mahmood and we're both prepared to excuse your earlier actions, since you must have been shocked by Dalia's death. But before I do such a thing, I must know if you had anything to do with this dishonorable and foolish thing Dalia did."

I remained still for a moment. My mind raced, trying to process the path I should take. Regardless of what happened, I had an obligation to defend Dalia's actions.

"Dalia did nothing wrong," I stated.

That one simple statement enraged him. He stepped toward me, shouting in a vile tone.

"Dalia did everything wrong! She dishonored her family by running around with that man. She was a whore! And for that she has fallen to a whore's fate! Do you think you know better than her own father? Now, I want to know if you had anything at all to do with this betrayal she orchestrated against her family and her home," he demanded.

"Any respect I may have had for Arab men or for Arab customs died with Dalia. I refuse to deny my beliefs any longer!" I

147

looked up at him before continuing, then threw submission to the wind.

"I will *not* be silent—I will not allow my silence to condemn her. Dalia did nothing wrong! I will defend her actions to my dying day. If you're here in search of an admission of guilt, or to look for incriminating details to substantiate your beliefs and her father's actions, you'll be disappointed. Whatever existed between Dalia and me will forever remain between us. She took her secrets to her grave, and I will do the same. I'll never agree with you about this, nor will I ever accept what her father has done. He's a murderer and you're his accomplice by justifying what he's done!" I burst out, just short of a scream.

He closed the small distance between us with lightning speed, and slapped my face hard.

"How dare you use that tone with me! How dare you call an honorable and just man like Mahmood a murderer in defense of a whore! I demand that you tell me what I want to know."

He raised his hand, prepared to strike me again. Then, from nowhere, my mother appeared and grabbed his arm.

"Mishan Allah [for God's sake], stop this. Let her rest. She's not in her right mind. For God's sake, leave her now, and after she's rested talk to her. I beg you, come with me, please, and give her time. You know how she loved Dalia. They were like sisters. Ever since they were young, they've been inseparable. Let her adjust to this news, I beg you. Pardon her words. It's anger that speaks now, not our Norma. I beg you, *la yumarie,* for my life, pardon her and give her time," she pleaded.

He snapped his arm, hurled my mother to the floor, and turned his spite toward her.

"Let go of me, *ya mara* [woman]. I warn you to keep your dis-

148

tance from this matter. Will you have me believe that she's distraught to the point of disrespect? Doesn't she realize that I gave her life, and I can take it from her for her defiant words alone!" he shouted.

My mother was now fighting for her life, as well as mine. She knew that only reasoned, respectful words had any hope of reaching my father and saving me, and she was doing the best and bravest thing she could do.

"Please, at this moment she doesn't realize the consequences of her words. I beg you, *ya habiby,* let's not lose our daughter for some hastily spoken words I'm sure she will regret once she has regained control. She's never been disrespectful toward you before. From that fact alone we should know that her anger is speaking now, not her heart. Please come with me," she said as she rose to her feet and put her hand out to him.

He angrily turned on his heel to face the door. "I will allow her a few hours of rest. But I demand an apology, and I demand that she go and apologize to Mahmood as well." And he strode out.

My mother sat on the bed and pulled me to her, holding my head on her chest and caressing my hair. She kept repeating *"Ya binty, ya binty, hutie himlik ala Allah, Allah bi himlik"* [my girl, my girl, put your troubles in God's hands, he'll carry you through this]. But I found little comfort in either my mother's arms or her words.

"I don't want God to carry me through this, I want him to take me away from here," I said.

"Oh, Norma, my baby girl, if you had anything at all to do with this, your father must never know. I know how much you loved Dalia, I loved her too, and I can't bear to lose you in the same way," she said.

"I can't keep quiet, Mom, that would make me as guilty as they are. Don't you see that Dalia did nothing wrong, and they killed her. They killed her for nothing."

"Norma, please, you can't go on defending her like this. Whether what she did was right or wrong doesn't matter anymore. Think of what Dalia would want. She wouldn't want you to die defending what she did. Please, Norma, you must apologize."

"I can't! I won't! Don't you understand, if I do that, I'll be just as guilty as they are. I won't condemn her by agreeing with them. I didn't condemn her in her life, and I'll be damned if I'll do it in death!"

"Norma, please think about what you're saying. If you don't apologize, it'll be suicide. What good can you do for Dalia if you're dead? I'm not saying that your apology must come from your heart, only from your lips. God and Dalia will know what remains in your heart."

"Mom, I'm no longer the same person. I won't give in to fear. I won't deny my heart and my beliefs. It's fear and silence that allows them to do this. How many more Dalias will die before someone stands up to them? Someone's got to fight for Dalia's innocence; it doesn't matter if I'm killed. I refuse to continue living this lie."

"Norma, sweetheart, you're not being rational. You can't do anything dead! I'm not asking you to live a lie; I'm asking you to stay alive. Do you think anything will change if they bury you too?"

"So you would rather have me live a lie?"

"I would rather have you alive under any circumstances!"

"Alive for what, to live as if I'm dead? What kind of life is that? What kind of life have you had? I refuse to spend the next twenty or thirty years with a forced smile on my face while my soul sheds tears of blood. I don't want to live longing for the freedom I will only find in death. That promise has pacified us—you!—too long.

I want to be free to live, really live, and do what I want. I want to believe what I want. If I can't have that, I have no life."

"Don't *say* that you can't have a wonderful life, you—"

"A wonderful life, you mean like you! You think I can't see past your smile to your broken heart? You think you can fool me into believing you're happy? I'm not Dad, I'm not my brothers; they don't see it because they don't want too, but I'm not blind. Didn't you ever have dreams? Needs? Goals?"

"Of course I did." She said it with a special tenderness that, for just that moment, was for the girl she had been, just like me, with dreams. "We all go through that confusing period in our lives, but we quickly learn our place and our responsibilities. You will too. This will pass, it will all pass, and—"

"It will not! I won't let it! I have goals and dreams. Dalia and I shared those dreams and now she's gone. My ties to this country and to these customs die with her! My dreams are of freedom, and my goal is to avenge her death. Nothing you or anyone else says will ever change that!"

"Norma, *habibati* [my love], I'm not trying to change what you believe, I'm only trying to keep you alive. I've said what I can; your life is in your own hands now. Understand that if they think for a moment that you had something to do with this, I can't save you. You have to calm down. I know it's not easy, and I pray that God gives you the strength and wisdom to choose your words wisely. I love you and I don't want to lose you. I'm sure that Dalia wouldn't want you to commit suicide, which is exactly what you'd be doing. Think carefully, my dear child. Apologize from your lips and save what burns in your heart. Don't waste your beliefs and passionate words on deaf ears. I beg you, say what they want to hear, and save your life. I'll let you rest now." Then she kissed me on the forehead and quietly left the room, leaving me to my confusion. My mother would never know the compassion, love, and sadness I felt for her.

I lay back down and thought carefully about everything my mother had said. I couldn't deny that she was right. My death would do no good to Dalia, and it would ensure that Mahmood got away with murder. If anything, my death would only help prove the accusations leveled against Dalia. I realized that I had to play by their rules for now. I tried to clear my head and rest. My body was rigid with tension, my muscles ached.

Then, suddenly, I thought of Michael. I had to warn him. He'd be next on their list. And I had to tell him about what had happened—that Dalia had been murdered, that he might be next. How could I reach him while my father had me under a microscope? I had just remembered . . . in order for Dalia's family to have the legal right to kill him, an autopsy had to be performed on Dalia first. If the results of the autopsy showed that she'd had premarital sex, nothing I or anyone else could do would spare Michael. If she was found to be a virgin, though, her family would risk years of a bloody family feud if they killed him. Although some families of honor killing victims ignore the law and kill the man involved regardless of the medical findings, I didn't believe that Dalia's family would take that route. I'd known them all my life, and I was sure that all they'd want to do is find a quick end to this embarrassment. I didn't doubt, however, that they'd kill Michael if the results were unfavorable, but I knew Dalia. I was sure that she was still a virgin.

I had to find a way to contact Michael and let him know what had happened. I hated having to be the bearer of bad news. But he had to hear it from me, no one else.

NINETEEN

When Dalia died, she was transformed, by the state and by Islam, into a body, to be handled by Jordan's system of laws and burial. But I could still feel her death only as a personal thing.

What had happened in the brief minutes, or seconds, of her death? Did her brothers join her father in pinning Dalia down as he stabbed her—or did they stab, too? Did she know she was about to be killed? Did she hear furtive sounds and padding feet coming toward her room as her breath stopped in terror? Or did they creep in as she slept and stab her in darkness? I have come to believe that her father, alone, wielded the knife. In the code of silence that surrounds an honor killing, I will never know for sure. But I will always be haunted by the possible scenarios, and cannot bear to think of Dalia if she were awake and knew what was moving toward her—if she saw the faces of her father, perhaps brothers, and a knife flashing toward her chest.

Did he, or they, feel anything for her as they struck? Or had their obsession with betrayal of honor turned Dalia into a faceless object of hate—had they so depersonalized her as an enemy of the codes they lived by that erasing her from the face of the earth was easy? Did Mahmood feel any guilt or remorse as he resisted calling an ambulance until he was sure his daughter was dead? And even if the brothers did not raise a knife, their support of the act makes them accomplices; Mohammed, who clearly betrayed Dalia to her father, is equally a murderer.

What is almost as hard to bear is the facelessness of her treatment after death. When the twelve stabbings were done and the knife pulled from her chest, her murder became a minor matter to be dispensed with swiftly in the Islamic courts that ruled on all religious or family matters. Hidden away from the light of the civil legal system, there would be no more punishment for her killer than the inconvenience of two or three hours before the Sharia's courts. There, male judges and juries, cheering this father in their hearts for upholding tradition, always sat with sympathetic ears for male murderers.

The police, no doubt, made their initial report of the incident before transporting Dalia's body to Palestine Hospital and noted that it was an honor crime. No crime scene would be taped off to protect the evidence. No murder weapons or other evidence would be collected. All her father would be required to do was to make a perfunctory appearance at court to testify about how Dalia had dishonored her family. If the court agreed that her actions warranted an honor killing, then he would receive the male judges' and jurors' respect and support for abiding by the ancient laws and having the courage to uphold his family's honor.

The laws pertaining to honor killings stem from ancient beliefs that, by now, have been codified into law. Because of this, someone charged with neglecting to wear a seat belt while driving faces stiffer penalties than the perpetrator of an honor crime. Where anyone found publicly criticizing the king automatically faces three years in prison, a man performing an honor killing spends less than three hours in front of the Sharia's courts.

Mahmood's court appearance would no doubt be scheduled for the following week. If I went and publicly defended Dalia's actions, I would certainly be killed. I wanted desperately to attend, but I knew that it would be almost impossible to get my father's permission to go. In the meantime, the hospital would perform the autopsy, and the results made available to the family and courts. It was vital that Michael be warned and remain hidden so he could survive until the autopsy results were available to the courts and prove that Dalia was still a virgin. The courts would then protect Michael. Dalia's father and brothers would face severe penalties if they tried to kill him. The "severe penalties," which are essentially fines, still might not be enough to stop them. Although I had believed that Dalia's family would choose to end this scandal quickly, I began to wonder if Michael should lie low for at least a week. I could find only one viable way to contact him.

I ran out of my room and burst into the living room to find my mother serving my father his tea. The room reeked of the apple-scented tobacco my father was steadily stuffing into his *argila* (water pipe). He sat in his black recliner, carefully poking and prodding the hot ashes with a tool to keep the *argila* lit as my mother knelt in front of him. Her head was lowered, and she carefully placed the hot mint tea on the end table nearest him before turning her attention to untying his shoes. He didn't acknowledge my entrance, but I knew he was waiting for me to honor the compulsory formalities.

"Excuse me. Forgive me for disturbing you. May I please sit down and talk to you for a moment?" I asked.

"Sit," he replied.

"*Yabba* [father], please forgive me. You're right, I was very disrespectful in my actions and my words, both to you and to Dalia's father." As I lowered my gaze, I caught my mother's glance and sensed her relief.

"Yes, you were. Until you answer my question, I cannot forgive you. Did you have anything at all to do with this scandal?" he asked sternly.

"Please, father, forgive me for my actions and words. I was very hurt and upset at the time and I lost control. And no, I had nothing to do with it," I said, keeping my gaze fixed on the floor. I didn't think I could deny my involvement if I had to look at him. I hated the words I was forcing out of my lips, and kept thinking, Please, God, forgive me, Dalia forgive me, but I have no other choice.

Paternal feelings were now so deeply buried that there was not a sign of relief in his face, as I'd seen in my mother's. Just the formal words.

"I'm glad to hear that you were not involved in this mess. I'll forgive you, but I expect you to apologize to Mahmood and his family as well. Understood?"

"Yes, Father. I'll go there right now, if you wish, and apologize."

"No, don't go now, it's getting late. It can wait till tomorrow. I'll take you then."

"As you wish, Father. May I ask something?"

"What is it?"

"I believe that I should go to the salon and put a notice on the door to let our . . . the customers know that it will be closed for a few days. I'd also like to get the appointment book so I can reschedule all of the appointments. If I may, I would like to do that tonight."

"Well, I suppose that's something that can't wait. I'll drive you once I've finished my tea."

"Thank you, Daddy, but I feel horrible about what I've done today. I've troubled you a lot, and I don't want to trouble you anymore. If it's all right with you, I'll ask one of my brothers to accompany me, or I can just walk there and do it quickly."

"No, I will not allow you to walk there alone at this hour. Amjed is in his room, have him take you."

"Thank you, Daddy. Again I apologize for disturbing you," I said as I stood up and slowly left the living room.

I stepped up the two half-circular white marble stairs that connected the living room to the long hall and went up the wide marble staircase on my way to Amjed's large and elegant room. These old houses handed down through the family had touches of grandeur, even if our middle-class life did not. As I walked, I went over phase two of my plan, calling on the conspiratorial skills well honed by the past year. By the time I stood outside Amjed's door, I believed I could pull it off.

My oldest brother, Amjed, and I were never very close. Preoccupied with his own world, he maintained only a distant interest in the events of my life. This distance meant that I had some respect and admiration for him, since he never meddled in my life, and so he never compounded my already complicated situations. I knocked on his door.

"Amjed, Dad said you have to drive me to the salon right now to pick up the appointment book and place a sign on the door." I said it boldly.

There was no answer.

"Did you hear me?" I yelled louder.

"Yes, yes, I hear you. Just give me a minute to change," he hollered through the door. "Okay, I'll be down in a second," he called, as I turned to leave.

I walked through the house in a daze, and poured myself a sip of tea in the kitchen as I waited for Amjed.

"Let's get this done quickly; I have plans tonight," he said as he appeared in the kitchen. I followed him out.

"I'll be quick, I promise. Thanks for taking me," I said as we stepped out into the cold, early evening air. I followed him to his car and prayed that the short drive would be silent. Once we were out of the driveway he turned to me and shattered the silence.

"I heard about what happened to Dalia. It's a terrible thing; she should have known better." The indifference in his voice angered me.

"It's more than terrible," was all I could say.

"You weren't involved, were you? You should know better."

"No. If you don't mind, I'm really not in the mood to talk about it," I said in an attempt to cut him off before I lost my composure.

"Well, I can understand that. So how long are you going to be?" he asked.

"Just a little while. You can wait in the car if you want," I replied, thankful that he'd changed the subject.

"Okay. I need to make some calls while you're inside," he said. We sat in silence the rest of the way.

He parked the car in front of the salon, pulled out his cell phone, and began making calls as I headed off into the salon. Once inside, I closed and locked the door and drew a shaky breath before flipping on the lights and rushing behind the front desk. I reached for the phone and suddenly realized that I couldn't remember Jehan's number—the same number I'd repeatedly dialed, week after week, for the past twelve months. It had vanished from my mind. I reached for the appointment book to search for her phone number. *I have to get hold of Michael!* was all I could think as I frantically flipped through the pages. If I took too long, Amjed would come to the door wondering what I was doing.

My anxiety and fear must have affected my eyesight. I was sure her number was in the appointment book and remembered writing it down myself, yet I was flipping through the pages for the fourth time and I couldn't find it. I closed the book and shut my eyes tightly.

Calm down, Norma, I told myself. Take your time and you'll find it. It's in here, just calm down. I started turning the pages more slowly. Take your time and you'll find it. It's in here, just calm down. Finally, of course, there it was. I reached for the phone.

As I dialed, I dreaded telling Michael about Dalia. This call would alter his life forever, just as it had mine, and I wasn't sure if I could stay composed long enough to say what needed to be said. I held my breath as the phone rang. A pleasant sounding, older woman's voice echoed through the receiver.

"*Marhaba*," she said.

"May I please speak to Jehan?" I asked.

"May I ask who's calling?" she replied.

"It's Norma," I said.

"Hold on a moment," she said. A few minutes later I heard Jehan's bubbly voice jump through the line.

"Hi, Norma. Is that you? How are you? What a surprise, I wasn't expecting to hear from you until next week. Are you okay?"

"Not so good. Something horrible has happened, and I need to talk to Michael. Is he there? Can you quietly get him to the phone?" I asked. My voice started cracking.

"What happened? Can I help?" she asked.

"No. I'm sorry, Jehan, but I really need to talk to Michael directly, and I'm pressed for time—he can explain it to you later," I replied.

"Okay, I'll get him as fast as I can," she said, and the line was silent.

Within seconds Michael's voice came on, the sound making what I had to say even harder.

I could hear concern and confusion in his voice as he asked, "What is it?" I started sobbing.

"I—It's . . . they . . . they . . . it's Dalia . . ." I managed to say between sobs.

"Dalia? What about Dalia? Norma, what's happened? They who? Please, Norma, calm down and tell me what happened. Is Dalia okay?"

"No, no, she's not okay! She's gone! She's gone, Michael. They took her away from us. She's gone," I kept repeating.

"What do you mean gone? They who? Norma, you're not making any sense. Gone where?"

"Gone. She's gone, and you . . . and they're going to want you next!"

"Norma, calm down. Calm down and tell me what you're talking about. They who?"

I took a deep breath and forced the words out.

"Michael, listen! It's Dalia's father, he found out about you. I don't know how—Mohammed, I think—but he did, and he killed her, and I think they're going to try to kill you too," I blurted out.

"No, Norma. No, it can't be true. What do you mean he killed her? It can't be. How? When? It can't be true, I don't believe it, it can't be," he said over and over again.

"Michael, it's true. He killed her this morning. They took her to Palestine Hospital. I saw her. I'm so sorry to have to be the one to tell you, but it's true."

"NO! God, no. Why, God, why? Oh, Dalia, no!" he cried into the phone, and the pain in his voice was almost more than I could bear. Please, God, I prayed, don't let Amjed come to the door right now.

"Michael, listen, you have to stay at the army base for a couple of days. You'll be safe there, in case they come after you."

"Norma, I can't believe what you're saying. There's nothing more they can do to me, they've taken my heart and my soul! If they want to collect my body, let them come," he said as he sobbed into the phone.

"Michael, no, please, you have to stay at the base. Do it for Dalia. Please, I can't lose you too. Please, Michael. We'll make them pay, I swear to you we will, but you have to make it through this, we both do. I need your help. Please, Michael, I can't do this alone. Please," I pleaded.

"I don't think I can live without her, I don't *want* to live without her. My Dalia, oh my God, why?"

"Michael, please, we'll make it through this together. I promise you." Amjed began honking and I knew my time was running out. Soon he'd come to the door. I had to hang up.

"Michael, Amjed's honking outside, I have to go, I have to hang up. Promise me, swear to me on Dalia, that you'll stay at the base for at least three days. Please."

"But where did you say they'd taken her?" he asked.

"No, Michael, please, you can't go there, promise me." Before I could finish Amjed was banging on the door.

"Promise me, Michael. Please. I'll keep in touch with you through Jehan. I'll let you know what's going on."

"I promise I'll stay at the base."

I hung up and ran to unlock the door.

"What's taking so long? Who were you talking to on the phone?" Amjed asked as he entered.

"I'm sorry, I didn't mean to . . . I was just calling tomorrow's appointments to cancel," I said, wiping tears with the back of my hands.

"Look, Norma, I realize that being in the salon is hard for you right now, but you'll get through this, and you'll soon realize that she brought this on herself."

I wanted to scream, but I knew I must keep quiet for now. I nodded my reply, afraid to open my mouth.

"Well, then, is there anything else you need to do before we leave?"

"Actually, if you could just write out a sign that says the salon will be closed until further notice and hang it on the door, I would appreciate it. In the meantime, I'll just grab the few things I need and then we can go."

"Yeah, sure, I can do that."

I walked back behind the counter, closed the appointment book, and handed him a blank piece of paper and a marker. Searching through the piles of notebooks and magazines on the desk, I set aside the appointment book, our scorebook, and unlocked the bottom drawer to take out our daily journal. This was the only thing that could prove Dalia even knew of Michael's existence. We'd spent years writing down our dreams, hopes, and fears, and through the diary Dalia would speak to me forever. I glanced in the direction of her station and remembered the day before our grand opening six years ago. She'd sat on the chair and I'd stood behind her, resting my head on top of hers, as we looked at each other in the mirror.

"Coffee?" I'd said.

"Cigarette," she shot back with a sly and brilliant smile.

The memory was so real, so alive, that I found myself smiling. I knew that N&D's would be closing permanently. This place had been our first timid step toward freedom, though it had felt bold at the time. What turn would my life take now? I grabbed my small pile of books and walked toward Amjed, who was taping the sign on the front door.

I handed him the keys and walked outside, took a deep breath as the cool wind slapped my face, then went to wait in the car as he turned off the lights and locked up.

From the passenger seat I watched as darkness began to descend on the city, blanketing the buildings, swallowing the streets, its thickness only broken by the occasional flickering streetlights. It would be a long and sleepless night. Tomorrow, I must restrain myself at least long enough to apologize to the one person I wanted to rip apart with my bare hands: Mahmood. That morning he had become my mortal enemy. Although I'd never felt the power of love that Dalia had felt, I'd believed that it was the strongest of all emotions. Now I was convinced that there exists another emotion that, once roused, surpasses the power of love, and could be, if not channeled properly, a totally destructive force: hate. I only hoped that I would have the wisdom to turn my hatred for Mahmood into something useful and not allow it to consume and destroy me. But I somehow needed this surge of hate to give me the strength to get through the next few weeks. Then I could begin looking for a way to avenge Dalia's death, and give her the peace she deserved.

As Amjed drove us home, I tightly hugged the books to my chest, relieved that I'd been able to warn Michael. But my relief was a drop of water in an ocean of grief. I prayed that God would give me the strength, wisdom, and patience to get through this day, this tragedy. But not even God could ever make me justify her loss. My mind began to waver between the reality of her loss and the fantasy of her return. Although I knew that I'd never see Dalia again, I also knew that I would never be able to let her go. Suddenly, my mind began to entertain a theory, a thought, really, that somehow, for no particular reason, offered me a tiny bit of comfort and made me feel less alone. Dalia would continue to live. While physically the finality of death is unquestionable, I believe I understood at that moment that death itself need not be final. After twenty-two years of friendship, I was left with a few photographs (taken secretly, since Islam does not allow women to have their pictures taken), and an endless film of memories. They would let me continue to touch and feel her vitality. Like millions before her, she would continue to live in the hearts and minds of all who loved her. I was strangely comforted knowing that, years from now, when I drank my morning coffee, she would come to me in the form of my memories. She would bring me a smile, a tear, a moment, and continue to confirm her existence.

TWENTY

As the blackness of night fell, at last, over the day of Dalia's murder—the longest day, I know, of my entire life—I curled up on my bed in a fetal position as I had that morning, knees pulled tight to my chest, while memories and images washed over me. I was trapped in the past, frozen on my bed, compelled by some mysterious energy to relive events as they replayed through my mind like a movie. Each memory ended with an image of Dalia deposited on that stainless-steel table, sheathed by the blood-spattered sheet. She was so tranquil and striking, like a resting seraph. Perfectly still. I slowly began to accept that she would never wake up.

When my sorrow became too great to handle without some kind of physical release, I forced myself to get up and walk about my room. I tried to clear my thoughts, but got tired looking for answers that didn't exist to questions that shouldn't have to be asked. I lay back down and the cycle began again. By daybreak, I was psychologically, spiritually, and physically drained. I forced myself to get out of bed, threw on some clothes, and went to the kitchen hoping that caffeine would give me the energy I needed to get through the day. As I slumped over the kitchen counter sucking down my fifth cup of coffee, my father came in.

"*Sabah al-khair, Yabba,*" I mumbled.

"*Sabah al-noor,*" he replied.

"Would you like some coffee?" I asked.

"Of course. Be ready around 3:30 this afternoon. I'll take you to Mahmood's then, and you can apologize to him and his family."

"Yes, Father, as you wish," I managed to reply between yawns.

"I'll have my coffee on the veranda," he said as he turned and left the kitchen. I put my head down on the counter and wished that the caffeine would kick in. Then I hauled myself to the stove and began making my father's coffee.

I waited on him silently and swiftly and went back into the kitchen, eager for him to leave. Once all of the men had gone to work, I moped around the house for a few hours, lost in my thoughts and careful to avoid my mother. By ten, it became impossible to dodge her any longer. She followed me from room to room, finally managing to trap me in the kitchen as I was brewing yet another pot of coffee.

"How do you feel today, *habibati?*" she asked, using the affectionate word that translates to a mother's honey, sweetheart, my love, my dear.

"Like the living dead."

"You look like you haven't slept at all."

"I didn't. I think sleep is a thing of the past."

"It'll get better. You'll see, time heals all wounds."

"This isn't a wound, this is my call to arms. My life here died with Dalia. I'm going to find a way out of this hell."

"Norma, honey, you're just upset. I'm not saying that the pain you feel now will disappear, but day by day it'll become easier to live with. I'm very proud of you for apologizing to your father."

"I said I was sorry because I knew I had no choice, but I have to tell you something, something I'm sure you already suspect. I was involved. I knew about it from the start and I helped her. That's why I'm so sure she did nothing wrong. I mean, according to all of you what she did was wrong, but all she did was follow her heart. She loved him, and loving him made her happier than I'd ever seen her. How can that be so wrong? She didn't hurt anyone."

"But she did. She hurt her family's reputation by being out with him, by even talking to him."

"That's ridiculous! I was there; I saw what happened. They were pulled to each other. I don't think either one of them could have escaped whatever force it was that brought them together. I saw it in their eyes. If their relationship was so wrong, then why did God allow them to meet in the first place? Do you know that she actually told me that she believed Michael was her destiny and that she couldn't live without talking to him? And she paid for loving him with her life."

"Norma, she was a big girl and she knew the risk she was taking. You should never have gotten involved. Anyway, we can't change anything now. The only thing we can do is make sure the same thing doesn't happen to you, and you've taken the first step by apologizing to your father and denying any involvement in this affair, and for that I'm proud of you."

"Proud of me for what? I'm not proud of myself. I feel as if I've betrayed Dalia. I feel like a coward. And today, I have to do it again by apologizing to the beast that murdered her. God, how I wish I could tell him what I really think of him, but I won't. I've realized that you were right about one thing; I can't do anything for Dalia if I'm dead. I don't know exactly when or how I'm going to avenge her death, but I know that no matter how long it takes or how hard it may be, I'll find a way, even if I die, too. I owe her that much, and I know that she'd have done the same for me."

"Sweetheart, you need to watch what you're saying. Your anger is speaking now. Dalia is only one of the thousands of women this happens to every year. I'm sure the others had mothers, sisters, and friends who were just as upset as you are now, but they realized, as you will in time, that nothing can be done about it. They suffer the loss in silence and then find a way to move on, as you will."

"No, I won't. I'm not like the rest, and neither was Dalia. But you don't have to convince me to suffer silently; I know it has to be that way for now. Look, Mom, I'm sorry, I don't mean to be rude or disrespectful, and I certainly don't want to take my anger out on you. I'm just an emotional wreck, I'm sorry. I love you and I understand that you're just trying to help me. Believe me, I do. But this is something you can't help me with, trust me."

"Just be careful. Whatever you decide to do, do it carefully. Just promise me that much."

"Don't worry, I'll be careful. Now, can I ask a favor?"

"Sure, what is it?"

"Can you call Dalia's mother and find out what they are planning to do next? Please, Mom, it's important to me. I have to know."

"Okay, I'll call her."

"Thank you so much, Mom. By the way, I need to confess one more thing. I smoke and I really need a cigarette. I have some hidden in my room. I'll just go grab one and be right back," I said as I stood up.

"You what?" she yelled.

Before she could continue, I bolted out of the kitchen and into my room. When I returned with the cigarettes, she stared at me and then at the pack of cigarettes before attempting to speak.

"I can't believe you smoke! How long have you been smoking? What else am I going to find out? You'd better not let your father find out, he'll kill us both."

"Oh, Mom, come on, it's no big deal. I've been doing it for years now. It's not that important. Just please make the call."

"For years! How could I have not known? Oh my God, why? How did you start?"

"Mom, please forget it now. Please make the call," I begged as I lit a cigarette and refilled my cup of coffee.

"All right, all right, but first go lock the door and put the chain on in case your father or one of your brothers comes home early. I don't want one of them to catch you with that filthy thing sticking out of your mouth."

"Thanks, Mom," I said, and kissed her cheek before running off to lock the doors. She followed me into the living room carrying the coffee and an ashtray. We sat on the love seat next to the phone. She picked up the phone and dialed the number as I sat and watched her. I listened to every word she said, my mind imagining what Dalia's mother was saying on the other end. After she said good-bye and before she could place the receiver down, questions burst out of my mouth.

"What's happening? What are they doing?"

"She said they're waiting for the report from the hospital."

"And then? What are they going to do then?"

"Well, if Dalia is not intact, they'll go after the young Catholic man."

"Do they know him? Do they know who he is? Are they going to try anything before the report is done?"

"Apparently Mohammed followed him home the day he saw the

two of them together, and he knows where he lives. It doesn't sound like they know him personally."

"Where's her father? Are you sure they're waiting for the autopsy?"

"Honey, I don't know. She said they're waiting for the autopsy, and will only do something if the results are negative."

"But are you sure? Where's Mahmood today? Is he home?" I asked, my fear mounting.

"No, *habibati*, he wasn't home. You know I can't ask her where her husband is."

"I know. What about the funeral? Are they going to have one? Can I go?"

"No, they're going to bury her in an unmarked grave. Her mother's very upset about that. They won't have any kind of service, so no one will be going."

"Oh my God! How could they? Oh, Dalia. Oh, Mom, how could they?" I said as I began sobbing. The thought of Dalia being buried all alone with no one to say good-bye to her disturbed me.

"Where? Where will they be burying her? I have to go. They can't just bury her like that. No service, no people . . . Oh my God, I can't believe they're going to do this."

"Calm down, my baby. There's nothing we can do. That's what Mahmood wants; there's nothing anyone can do. I'm sure it'll be in the big cemetery just outside the city."

"When? What day?"

"Well, the coroner will move her body there once the hospital has completed the exam. The earliest it could be is the day after tomorrow."

"The hospital should know, shouldn't they? I have to know, I

170

have to be there. She can't be buried alone. Mom, please, I have to find out. Can I call the hospital?"

"Sweetheart, even if you call the hospital and find out, I don't think your father will allow you to go."

"He has to. Please, Mom, I have to be there. Please, you have to help me, I'm begging you," I pleaded.

"Yes, yes, all right. Just calm down. Go ahead and call the hospital. I'll let you go, but we must be careful that your father doesn't find out."

"I know. Thank you, Mom. And Mom, please understand, I don't want to do what I'm about to do behind your back, so I'm going to tell you. I have to call Jehan, Michael's sister. Michael is the Catholic man. I have to let her know that Mahmood may be on his way there."

"Oh, Norma, I don't know if that's such a good idea. I don't want you to get involved in this any further. What if your father finds out?"

"Mom, please. Mahmood has already killed Dalia, and I won't stand by and watch him kill Michael, too. They didn't do anything, and you'll see that I'm telling you the truth once the autopsy results are out. Would you rather I stay quiet and have them kill him? He's the same age as Amjed; how would you feel if something like this happened to him, and he was killed for nothing?"

"Okay, dear, I'll let you make this one call, but that's it. Warn him and that's it. Do you *hear* me? If your father ever finds out about this, we're both dead. Don't you dare speak to him on the phone, only his sister, and lose that number after today," she commanded.

"Thank you, Mommy. Thank you. You've helped me save an innocent man's life. You'll see, trust me."

First I called the hospital to get the update I needed, and that I knew Michael would want.

"Palestine Hospital. How may I direct your call?" The receptionist's high-pitched, nasal voice jangled abrasively into my brain. Was my sensitivity due to lack of sleep and an overdose of coffee, or just a normal response to an irritating voice? I held the earpiece away from my head as I spoke into the mouthpiece.

"I need some information, please. My sister is in your hospital. She passed away yesterday morning, and my family and I were wondering when the hospital would complete the postmortem and release the body."

"Well, miss, you'll have to speak to the morgue. Hold on a moment while I transfer you. I'm sorry for your loss. One moment," she said routinely. I heard a few clicking sounds, and a man's voice.

"Morgue. How can I help you?"

"Yes, my sister died yesterday, and she's there now. I was wondering . . . We're waiting for a postmortem exam to be completed. When will that be done, and when will the hospital release the body for burial?" I asked.

"Oh yes, I remember her. Hold on a minute, let me check . . . she's your sister, you said?"

"Yes, yes, my sister."

"I'm sorry for your loss. Hold on a minute. Okay, here it is. Let's see, we were told the body would go directly to the cemetery in Rajib after the autopsy, which is scheduled for tomorrow. It looks like we'll be taking her the following day as it'll be too late to take her after the exam."

"Do you know what time of day you'll be transporting her?"

"Well, she'll probably go out with the morning drop-offs. I'm sorry, that doesn't sound right. I think she'll be at the cemetery around nine in the morning. I really am sorry for your loss, miss. My condolences."

"Yes, thank you. Thank you so much, you've been very helpful."

I sat staring at the phone after I'd hung up.

"Well, what did they say?" my mother asked, breaking my trance.

"They said that she'll be at the cemetery in Rajib the day after tomorrow. So that's . . . wait, what day is it today, it's . . ."

"It's Thursday."

"So Saturday at nine. I have to be there, Mom. I have to find a way to be there."

"Well, you can worry about that later. If you want to make that other call, you'd better do it quickly."

I watched my mother out of the corner of my eye as I reached for the phone. I wondered what she'd experienced to make her so understanding now. I knew that this wonderful woman had spent her life doing her best to portray an image of happiness, yet I wondered if she'd ever felt genuine joy. I tried to picture my mother at my age and decided that at some point she must have entertained the same hopes I did. I wondered if she'd suffered a loss like mine. Surely she'd had a life before becoming a wife and mother, though she never shared many details of it. It was as if parts of that existence had vanished, and others were filed away in the secret compartments of memory. As a child, I'd spent countless hours watching her, trying to translate my mother's private expressions. Yet I remained baffled.

I realized that I was as close to my mother as she'd ever allow anyone to be. She maintained an emotional distance as a form of self-preservation, it seemed, a barrier she built to protect her soul—and perhaps any surviving shred of the unique and independent person who had been forced underground at age ten—

from the harshness of reality. I wondered what kind of pain she had endured to build her fortress, and I ached at the thought of her suffering, as I knew she was aching as she watched mine. Watching her, I decided that it must have been that pain that bound her to live within these borders. I wondered whether the grief I was feeling now would force me to do the same.

"You'd better hurry and make that call," she said, her voice bringing me back from my thoughts. Seconds later, I had Jehan on the phone.

"Norma? Hold on a second." Her muffled voice called out, "I've got it, Mom, it's for me. Can you please do me a favor and get the notebooks I left on the desk in my room?"

"Norma? Sorry, I had to get her out of here. My God, Michael told me what happened. I can't believe it. It's so terrible, so unbelievable. I'm so sorry. How are you holding up?"

"Not so great. How's Michael?"

"Not good. He's still in his room; he didn't even want to get up this morning. This really hit him hard. He loved her so much."

"I know he did, so did I. But Jehan, you have to get him out of there. Dalia's father isn't home. He could be on his way to your house; he knows where you live. You have to get Michael out of there now. Especially if your father's not home."

"My dad's gone. He leaves before seven. I'll do my best to get Michael out of here."

"Please, do whatever you have to. Tell your mother, call your father, I don't care, if you don't get him out of there you could lose a brother, and I'll lose another friend to Mahmood's insanity. And Jehan, tell him to stay at the base for the next three days or so." He'd obviously been too distraught yesterday to care about safety and had ignored my previous urgings.

"I will, I promise. I love him so much and I don't want anything to happen to him. Have you heard anything else?"

"All I know is that she'll be taken to the cemetery in Rajib on Saturday morning. It's supposed to be an informal funeral; the bastard isn't even going to give her a service and, according to her mother, none of her family is allowed to go. I'll try to arrange it so we can go, but I'm worried that her father will show up. Don't tell Michael about the funeral yet, at least not until I figure out a safe way for us to be there. I have to hang up now. Take care of him, Jehan. He's going to need your help. He loves you and I know he'll listen to you. I'll call you if I find out anything else."

"Take care of yourself, too. Be careful. Thanks for calling. Good-bye."

I hung up the phone and lit another cigarette before turning to face my mother.

"I didn't hear you tell her about Dalia. How does she know that Dalia's been killed? Did you call them before?" she asked.

"Yes, I did. I wanted to be the one to tell Michael about Dalia, and I had to warn him of the danger."

"But how? From where? When?"

"Last night from the salon."

"Does Amjed know about all of this?"

"No, he was in the car. Don't worry, I was careful."

"Norma, this is a dangerous game you're playing. I don't think you should contact him again. You've done all you can. He's been told and warned, now you must walk away."

"Mom, please, I can't back away, not now, not until this is over. I can't talk about it anymore. I really need to go lie down for a while. I feel like I'm about to pass out."

"Try to get some rest and I'll wake you when your father comes home."

"Actually, could you wake me up at three? I have to be ready to leave with Dad. He's going to take me to apologize to Mahmood today."

"Well, then, at least eat something. Remember, you have to control yourself over there."

"I'm not hungry. My stomach feels like it's doing flips. I just need some rest, that's all."

"Honey, you didn't eat yesterday either . . . just let me make you a—"

"No, Mom, but thanks. Thanks for all your help, and for understanding. I love you," I said as I embraced her and turned to leave.

"I love you too, don't ever forget that. You're my precious, my only daughter. I'm just so worried about you." She tried to look stern. "By the way, we'll be discussing your smoking when this is all over."

"I know, believe me I know. Thanks for waiting," I shot back as I left the room.

I lay on my bed, but there was no escape. My mind and body felt like battered casualties of war. I was too exhausted to think clearly, and would have welcomed amnesia. But I had to remain focused on what I had to do. A little while later, my mother roused me, and I dressed quickly and followed her downstairs to find my father in the living room.

"I finished early, so we'll go to Mahmood's now. Let's go," he ordered.

In a few minutes we were walking up to Dalia's door and her mother, eyes still swollen and red, was escorting us into the living room. My father busied himself, making all the formal greetings, shaking hands, and kissing everyone on the cheek. I just walked in and planted myself on a seat in a corner. I sat in a daze, my eyes refusing to blink. I kept expecting Dalia to walk in and begin her greetings, as she had for twenty years. Then I heard my father's voice as if it came from an echo chamber, and my name.

"Norma. Norma, don't you have something you'd like to say to Mahmood and his family?"

I remained still.

"Norma. Norma . . ." he repeated.

"Yes, yes, I do," I heard myself say. My voice sounded alien. I looked around the room and saw that everyone was staring at me. I caught sight of Dalia's mother and her eyes begged me to tread cautiously. Mahmood, the object of my loathing, was sitting on the couch across from my chair, his beloved hunting trophies above him—the stuffed birds and small animals on the wall staring at me. Mahmood, I sensed, wanted me to make a mistake and say something that would jeopardize my life. I could feel the anger he still felt toward Dalia now directed toward me. His stare ignited a spark of fear that risked overtaking the emotions I was trying so desperately to control. I shut my eyes tightly, running through the speech in my mind.

"Well, Norma, we're waiting. What do you have to say?" my father broke in, commanding me to speak.

"Yes . . . I . . . Yes, I have something to say regarding my behavior yesterday. I was truly shocked and very hurt. Regardless of the fact that I couldn't and wouldn't, and probably never will, believe that Dalia deserved such a fate, I had no right to disrespect you or your family, and I apologize. I didn't mean in any way to doubt your decision or judgment."

I paused and looked at Mahmood before continuing on to more dangerous ground.

"And I suppose I owe you an apology for my loving your daughter like a sister, and finding her loss unbearable and your apathy over her loss infuriating. If so, I apologize for being human. I'm afraid that our God has created me with a very low threshold for pain, and I lost control. I envy your strength, Mahmood, for upholding your family's honor. After all, what is a life in the face of honor? I suppose that because I'm not a man, I can't comprehend such apathy, such disregard for human life. I'm sure you must be right. I mean, what can a woman know or understand about a man's honor? After all, it's a man's place to control and maintain the code we must live by. And I guess Dalia, in your eyes and in your mind, stepped outside the boundaries. You had the strength to do what needed to be done, and there's no room for emotion in honor, I suppose."

I was stunned by the strength and clarity I had managed to find. It seemed to be coming from somewhere beyond me, as if Dalia was squeezing my arm, urging me on. I was nearly done.

"So you see, I truly envy your indifference, because I'd love to be free of the crippling pain I feel. I'd love to be able to say that I feel nothing, but I'd be lying. The truth is that my world was shattered the moment you took her life, but I know that's my problem. Again I apologize, because, regardless of the fact that what you did tore my heart from my chest, I didn't have the right to disrespect you or your family in your home. The simple truth remains the truth, she was your daughter before she became my friend, and who am I to defy your wishes? I'm nothing more than a grieving friend, and I ask for your forgiveness for my loss of control."

Everyone sat silently for what seemed like an eternity, each with a baffled look on his or her face. Dalia's mother was the only one who shared in the tears I couldn't keep from erupting when I'd finished. Mahmood was clearly trying to assess my words and decide whether I'd made an adequate apology or a series of criticisms with a mock apologetic tone. My father was the first to break the silence.

"Well, as you can see, she's truly sorry, and I can assure you that she had nothing to do with Dalia's betrayals." I knew that my father was in a difficult position, since the purpose of this visit was to show that he had control over me. He had no choice but to insist that he did, or he would look like a fool.

"Yes, well, that was quite an apology," commented Mahmood.

"It's obvious that she's still mourning the sudden loss," replied my father.

"In light of that fact, I'll forgive her for her actions yesterday, and I hope that our families can remain close."

As soon as I heard these words, I jumped into the conversation before my father had a chance to say anything else. Mahmood's words were a slap in the face. His nerve . . . suggesting that our families remain close. I wasn't authorized to respond as a representative of my family, but I could speak for myself and I would be damned if I would ever speak to this murderer after today.

"With all due respect, I believe that my only tie to your family was Dalia. As far as I'm concerned, the only thing we have left to discuss is the salon. I've reached a decision about that. I refuse to work there any longer, so I suppose that gives you and my father something to discuss. I would like to say, with my father's permission, that I'd like to go there and pick up my personal belongings tonight," I said, looking at my father.

"We can discuss that later," my father replied with disapproval. I realized that he was upset that I'd voiced my decision about the salon publicly, before discussing it with him. But I decided that since I'd discussed only "my" connection to Dalia's family, he shouldn't be angry. I waited for a few moments before speaking again.

"I guess that completes all I came for." Then I turned to my father. "If you don't mind, Father, may I wait for you in the car?"

Dalia's mother stood up and began saying, "No, no, let me bring some coffee, you didn't even drink anything, please, sit down."

I politely refused the coffee, and turned to my father once again, my eyes pleading for a release.

"*Yala, imsha,* go ahead, I'll be out shortly," he finally said. I started toward the door, but before I could leave the living room, Mahmood called out.

"Actually, I have some questions that I would like you to answer before you leave."

"I'm sorry, Mahmood, but as I've already pointed out, I no longer have any ties to you or your family, and so I'm in a rather difficult position. I'm not allowed to speak to men who are not related to me. I'm sure you can understand that, as I'm only living by the same laws you used to condemn Dalia. Therefore, I'm afraid any questions you have will have to be directed to my father."

"The questions I have cannot be answered by your father. They must be answered by you," he insisted.

"Well, forgive me then, Mahmood, but it seems as if you've placed yourself in a difficult position. I have no answers for you. Your daughter should have answered your questions before she died. You'll have to bury any remaining questions along with her. Now, if you'll excuse me," I said and continued walking toward the exit at a slow pace.

"Abu Amjed, I must insist that you tell her to answer my questions," he commanded. I stopped walking and waited for my father, who again found himself in an awkward position. If he forced me to answer Mahmood's questions, it would look as if he wasn't sure of my innocence, which would only make him, again, look a fool. In this cool and formal exchange, two Arab men were sparring fiercely for their honor.

"I'm sorry, Mahmood, but I believe my daughter is absolutely correct. I have already guaranteed that she was not involved, and so I can't imagine what questions she could answer. Therefore, I must insist that you direct any inquiries to me. Norma, go wait in the car."

"Abu Amjed, am I to believe that you are protecting your daughter, helping her to hide the truth?"

"I've nothing to protect her from. I'm only insisting that she abide by my rules."

"But I'm not convinced that she had nothing to do with this, and I think she should answer some questions to prove her innocence. I'd imagine that you would want the same thing," Mahmood stated.

"I'm not the one who doubts her, Mahmood. Your behavior makes me question whether it's my daughter's innocence you doubt or your daughter's guilt."

As soon as I heard these words, I stepped outside. I knew that I'd won the first battle, but I also knew that the war was far from over.

I ran out and waited for my father in the car. I was positive that my father had protected me for his own sake, not mine. If he agreed with Mahmood, it would look as if he couldn't handle his own daughter. My father was always the image of politeness when he was in public, and I'd never heard him use the tone he'd used tonight except in our own home. I assumed that he'd been insulted by Mahmood's requests. Whatever his motive, I loved it.

Once home, I locked myself in my room and tried to think of a way to go to Dalia's informal funeral with Michael. I knew that I could rely on some help from my mother. Together I trusted we'd pull it off.

That evening, my mother came into my room carrying a tray of food and juice.

"You have to eat something. Why don't you come downstairs?" she said.

"I can't, Mom. I'm thinking of Dalia's funeral, of how I can go and—"

"Stop *now!* I told you I'd help you. Forget it now and rest. Rest your mind before you're too sick to go anywhere."

"Mom, please do me a favor? Don't say anything to Dad about the funeral."

"I won't . . . just eat something," she said as she left the room.

I needed to be certain of every detail for Saturday. In case Mahmood was watching from afar, it would be wiser if Michael and I didn't show up together, confirming Mahmood's suspicions.

I slept through the night, and most of Friday, getting up only to call Jehan and tell her my plans for the funeral.

On Saturday, I rose with the sun and dressed in black, while I waited for my father and brothers to leave the house. Then I kissed my mother good-bye, reassuring her that all would go well, and left for my final appointment with Dalia.

Rajib is a tiny village in the outskirts of Amman, just off the road to Sabah. The village is so tiny that it can't be found on any maps. The only reason it's known to anyone beyond its inhabitants is that an ancient myth is said to have taken place there. It's a legend mentioned in both the Bible and the Koran. Seven Christian boys were being persecuted, and they escaped to a cave where they slept for over three hundred years. This "cave of seven sleepers" or Ahl Al-Kahf [cave of the people] is next to the main mosque in Rajib. Dalia would be laid to rest between the mosque and an old Byzantine cemetery 500 meters to the east.

The place, as a whole, was bizarre. The two burial grounds, one Christian and one Muslim, were next to a site both religions consider holy. I always thought that it was odd that Muslims, who spent most of their lives trying to avoid deep personal relationships with Christians, considered it acceptable to lie next to them for all eternity. I determined to see it as a sign of future unity between the two faiths, a time of religious accord. Holding on to that theory, I hoped, would make the desolation of the place easier to tolerate.

I arrived at the cemetery and watched the men bury her from a distance. She would have no coffin—part of the harsh end for honor-crime victims. Her body was placed into a freshly dug hole. Workmen shoveled the brownish red dirt over her, then placed a crude cement slab on top, covering the dirt. These grunting men were the only witnesses at her graveside. No flowers or tears were left on this unmarked grave, only the aura of shame.

When the workmen left, I walked to the site and stood beside her grave. Michael appeared out of nowhere and stood next to me.

"What are you doing here?" I asked.

"I didn't want to wait. And besides, I think that she would want both of us at her side, don't you?" he replied.

"Yes, but what if someone sees us?"

"Don't worry, Jehan is looking out for us."

I slowly knelt beside Dalia's grave, my knees pressed on the sharp-edged gravel stones, and reached out to touch the unmarked cement rectangle that covered the spot. Clumps of the red earth spilled up over the edges of her grave onto the cold gray stones. It was the only evidence that this grave was new. Michael and I knelt by her side, silently saying our good-byes, mourning our loss, sharing our sorrow. We sat there for several hours, undisturbed, until he broke the stillness.

"Damn him for taking her from me."

"I know," was all I could reply.

"We have to do something about this. There has to be *something* we can do."

"We will, Michael. I promise, we will," I whispered.

TWENTY-ONE

*T*he blistering midday sun beat against the rooftops of the city as I sat on the veranda, slowly sipping endless cups of coffee, alternately buried in a book and gazing in the direction of Dalia's home. In the months since Dalia's death, this was how I'd spent my days. Time seemed to have stopped. I hadn't returned to the salon since the day Mohammed had picked up Dalia's things and left me there to sort through mine. The rooms had looked so bare without Dalia's possessions, and her presence. I had gathered my belongings quickly and left, locking the door one final time, cutting my link to the dreams and plans we'd shared there.

I was now a hermit, leaving the house only by force or out of absolute necessity. I'd lost interest in everything but books, the only physical objects that seemed powerful enough to transport me to some other place and time. I hungered to escape, to visit different worlds, see other ways of life, and go to places where Dalia could have lived safely with Michael, or where I could more happily keep her alive in my mind. No one here truly understood me, or my pain, though my mother tried. But she was a generation away. Seeing her less visibly upset than I was made her seem worlds apart.

The one person who understood and shared my grief was Michael. I knew, though, that it was growing increasingly danger-ous to stay in touch with either him or Jehan. It was only a matter of time before Dalia's father and brothers found out that Jehan was Michael's sister. Once they made that connection, they'd assume that, since I'd hired her to work at the salon, I was involved in the conspiracy. Dalia's father had started dropping by our house at least once a week. I could tell by his words and the tone of his voice that he was now determined to prove that I'd been involved. I knew I'd created this; he hadn't liked my apology speech and was angry that my father now questioned Dalia's guilt. I had to be par-ticularly careful, but that was easy, for my depression was pulling me further and further down and I was no longer interested in see-ing my friends.

But Michael and Jehan were not willing to go away. Michael made Jehan call me almost every day, just to make sure I was still alive. After losing Dalia, he became obsessed with the safety of all the women he knew, and was particularly worried about me since he knew I was fully capable of speaking my mind. He constantly asked Jehan to warn me to keep my mouth shut. He felt it his duty to protect the one other person Dalia had loved as much as she loved him.

In the first few weeks after her death I tried to support Michael and, for a while, I worried that he was the one with the death wish. The tables seemed to have turned now and he was supporting me. All his warnings and encouragements were wasted. The only thing that might have sprung me from my depression was a plan for revenge, or a report that Mahmood had been the victim of a fatal or crippling tragedy.

Nothing of the kind happened. Mahmood, I learned, had been

186

released on bail after turning himself in to the police. At his so-called trial, he was found guilty of a misdemeanor and sentenced to three months in jail, but immediately released based on the time he'd served out on bail—in the comfort of his own home—awaiting trial.

This particular Monday morning had started routinely enough. Cleaning the house, sitting on the veranda. I was lying on my bed reading a book about the history of ancient Greece when the phone rang. As I dragged myself down the stairs, thinking it was Jehan, I heard my mother answer, extend the customary formal greetings and wishes of good health, and ask the caller to hold on.

"Jehan's on the phone, dear."

"Norma, we need to talk." A man's voice burst through the phone.

"Michael! What are you doing on the phone? If my mom finds out that we're talking, she'll kill me," I whispered.

"Don't worry, you don't have to talk, just listen. I've found a way to get you out of Jordan. I can get your paperwork done; passport, visas, and everything else. I can get you a visa for either England or Greece. Before you start to object, listen to what I have to say. You must leave Jordan! Your life is in danger here! I know that you're not fighting the way you did in the beginning, but your grief will turn to anger again, and when it does, they'll kill you! They won't excuse you this time. They won't wait for an apology. They'll kill you. Do you understand me? I don't want to lose you, too. You have to leave. I promise that I'll keep trying to change things here. I'm working with the head of a women's group, and we'll continue to do all we can to change the laws. But I'll feel much better if you're out of the country. All I need you to say is yes or no."

Michael knew that I'd vowed to work for Dalia's dream of equal

187

rights and freedom for women in Jordan and so he assumed that I'd refuse to leave the country. I thought about all the things he'd said and instantly knew he was right. The moment I defended Dalia publicly, spoke out in her defense, I'd be guilty enough to warrant an honor killing. I knew that to make any kind of difference, I'd have to do it from thousands of miles away. I wouldn't survive long enough in Jordan to be heard. I had to leave in order to be free to speak, and to be heard. He was right. The only solution was to leave Jordan.

"Yes, I'll do it. But how? I mean I think my answer is yes, but we have to discuss all of the details. I can't say much now. Meet me tomorrow at the Books Café at six," I whispered into the phone while looking around to make sure my mother wasn't listening, and then hung up. I went back to my room, carefully avoiding my mother, afraid that she'd see that I was up to something.

※

I spent that night perched on the edge of my bed, reviewing Michael's words. They had resurrected the anger my grief and depression had been masking for the past few months. I'd done nothing to keep my promise to Dalia, while Mahmood had gotten away with murder. I'd promised she wouldn't die in vain. I knew that Michael was right; I had to leave before I lashed out at either Mahmood or my father. I didn't care where I went—anywhere but Jordan. But what would I do once I got there? I would be alone, with no Dalia, Michael, mother, relatives, or friends—and no hope of returning to Jordan, ever. I was afraid of leaving the only world I knew, afraid of the unknown.

The months I'd spent living like a hermit had been by my father and brothers' estimation a kind of penance—proof that I had nothing to hide, and no secretive contacts going on. Getting one of my brothers to leave me at the bookstore for a few hours would not be a problem. Amjed had already agreed to drive me as soon as he came home from work. When I heard his car outside, I bolted out the front door and jumped in.

"Are you sure you have everything you need? Do you have enough money?" he asked as he drew a fifty dinar bill from his wallet and handed it to me. "Take this in case." How sad that my response to a generous gesture from my brother was only suspicion.

At Books Café, I found Michael lurking around one of the shelves. We walked around the store for the two hours, picking up books and flipping through them as we talked. He explained how he would get my passport and visa issued, using my ID, which I gave him. He suggested that I go to Greece, because he was closer to his friends there than his friends in London. He spent the remainder of the time trying to reassure me that all would go well. If all went as planned, he predicted that I'd be in Greece the following month. He even offered to pay all of my expenses. I hesitantly agreed because I knew that my savings were running low and I realized that I wouldn't be able to scrape much more together before my departure. By the time Amjed pulled up to the curb, I'd agreed to go ahead with the plan, given Michael my ID, and bought a pile of six books.

"Did you find everything you were looking for?" he asked as I closed the door and positioned myself in the car.

"I did," I replied.

For the rest of the month I got updates on Michael's progress from Jehan. In the meantime, I distanced myself even further from my family, worried that if I got too close they'd figure out my secret. My feelings about leaving changed daily. On one hand, I was excited and couldn't wait to see another country and experience another way of life. On the other hand, I was angry because I felt as if I were being exiled from my homeland simply because I didn't condone honor killing. It seemed ridiculous that in order to try to make a difference in Jordan, I had to leave, and although I knew I had no other choice, I constantly second-guessed my decision.

ॐ

Finally Jehan gave me a date, time, and flight number, and told me that Michael would meet me at the airport, posing as my oldest brother. Now the only thing left to do was to arrange a way to be at the airport on time. I would be flying to Athens in a few days. My flight was scheduled for eleven on the morning of May 10.

That morning, I dressed, threw a few things into a gym bag, and ran down to my mother after my father and brothers had left for work.

"Mom, I have to get something from the salon and drop a few things off. Can I go?" I asked.

"Why don't you wait until your father gets home? I don't even have the keys," she replied.

"Mom, this really can't wait and it may take me a while. I just want to go through a lot of the things I left there. I still have a set of keys."

"Just have some breakfast first."

"Actually, Mom, I want you to have some breakfast with me. We can eat on the veranda, okay?"

She brightened. "It's nice to see you starting to become active again."

"You go and sit on the veranda and I'll serve you breakfast, *please*. It would make me happy."

"Well, all right," she agreed. I struggled to keep from crying as I cooked and carried the food out to her. This was the last time we'd sit here having breakfast together, perhaps ever. I sat staring at her, trying to create a permanent memory of this moment. Oh, how I wished I could take her with me, or tell her that I was leaving, but she would become too emotional. And it would put her life at risk; my father would kill her if he thought she'd known anything about my escape. After breakfast, I hugged her tightly and kissed her repeatedly on both cheeks.

"What's all that for? You're acting as if I'm never going to see you again," she said. I could scarcely speak.

"I love you, Mother. I want to thank you for everything."

"Well, I love you too, and I'm so glad you're feeling better."

I left my father's house and walked toward the salon, as I had so many mornings before, often with Dalia by my side. This time I noticed every pebble, every tree, every detail. It would be the last time I'd ever walk down these streets. Or see my mom.

I was a little girl again, ready to run back to the safety of my mother's skirts and arms. I realized that was the only thing I couldn't bear to leave. If only a generation could fall away, and she could run from the house and join me, arm in arm, as we walked to freedom.

§

I arrived at the airport to find Michael waiting outside. He ran toward me as I stepped from the taxi.

"Thank God you made it. I was worried you'd change your mind," he said.

"I gave you my word. I'm ready to leave."

He checked me in and waited with me until they began boarding my flight to Athens.

"This is it. You're going to be safe now, and you'll be free. Don't worry about anything. When you get there, take a taxi to the address I gave you, they're expecting you. God be with you," he said.

"Thank you, Michael, thank you for everything. In a few days or so will you please contact my mother and tell her that I'm okay? Don't tell her anything else, just that I'm okay. Please?"

"I will. I promise. Don't worry."

I boarded the plane and, as it took off, I wept. I cried out of joy and fear. I cried for my mother, and for the empty seats that should have been Dalia's and Michael's. I cried for the stark rosy beauty of the desert, the mystique of Aqaba, even the gossips in the salon who had no hope of ever having anything bigger or better to do. I cried for my father, as trapped in his prison of laws, pride, and obligations as my mother.

And I thanked God that I was lucky enough to be escaping. I had no idea what would happen to me. Only that whatever I found would be better than what I had left, where—for how many generations more?—exuberant, idealistic innocents like Dalia faced the daily possibility of death.

AFTERWORD

*H*onor crimes have been an accepted part of Jordanian culture since the beginning of the human record. These crimes are committed in other countries as well, but it is difficult to say how frequently, since most countries don't keep statistics about the number of deaths caused by this barbaric ritual. The idea of murder as a way to cleanse family honor is said to be most common in Jordan and among Palestinians, where it is firmly rooted in ethnic Bedouin tradition, which is still as pervasive as a desert sandstorm even in urbanized Arab families. Using just the published figures, each week one Jordanian woman is murdered for losing her chastity, whether she's a victim of rumor or a victim of rape. As with Dalia, the mere suspicion that she has lost her virginity can lead to a girl's, or woman's, murder.

Similar to most cases, suspicion alone was all Mahmood needed to sentence Dalia to death, and although the autopsy report proved she was still a virgin and his suspicion of her immoral behavior was unfounded, he never showed regret or remorse over his actions. He, along with her brothers, defended his actions by claiming that the fact she had any contact with Michael at all was enough to tarnish their family's honor, and therefore she deserved death.

Many honor killings, however, are later classified as suicides or accidental deaths, and so the published figures are very unreliable. The most frequent, and mistaken, claim is that these murders are born of Islamic faith, when in fact the murders are a cultural hangover of the tribal life that predated both Islam and Christianity. True, Islamic law subjugates women and calls for "scourging" rule breakers, but the code of honor killings has its roots in the Hammurabi and Assyrian laws from 1200 B.C., which declared a woman's chastity to be her family's property. These were the laws evolved from an unforgiving desert, common to all Arabs of the region, of whatever faith. These days, Christian women are just as likely to be killed as Muslim women for "dishonoring" their families.

There are two reasons why Jordan has gone to great lengths to keep this dirty secret tucked away from public view, and has largely succeeded. First, it hurts the image they're promoting to the Middle East and to the world of a modern democratic state. To Westerners, honor killings are seen as an exotic, scarcely believable, anthropological phenomenon that appears only in a few rare, isolated, still-primitive pockets—like head-hunting in New Guinea. While writing these words (on May 17, 2002), I spotted a long story in the *New York Times* and on the Web about a woman from a primitive village in "the barren northwest" of Pakistan near the Afghanistan border who has been condemned to death by stoning for being forcibly raped by her brother-in-law; a victim, said the *Times*, of "Pakistan's strict Islamic laws." Jordan does not want to be linked in the media's mind with these backward, desolate cultures.

Second, there is real fear that the issue is a time bomb whose fuse could be lit by fanning public sentiment against the practice. And so Jordan discourages any stories about honor killing in the media. Hints of the subjugation of women do appear, but—as with a story that appeared in the *Times* on the same day as the story of the Pakistani woman—as a tiny two-inch story about Toujan Faisal, the only woman ever elected to Jordan's parliament, being sent to prison for speaking out against government corruption. The fact that she was the first and only woman in that all-male body is a revealing story of repression in itself!

ॐॐ

And so Jordan continues to be reluctant to discuss this issue, and its officials are unwilling to provide accurate statistics and information about today's honor crimes. Some government officials claim that 25 percent of all murders each year are honor crimes, while others try to say that only about twenty-five women are murdered annually for reasons of honor. The Public Security Director, Major General Thaher Fawaz, said that in 1999 there were a total of 61,523 crimes in Jordan; of these 5,173 were classified as felonies (since honor crimes are categorized as misdemeanors, they are not included in this number), 2,248 were drug related, and the remaining 54,102 were either burglary (depending on the nature of the offense, this is sometimes considered a felony), assault and battery (usually domestic violence where the victim is female), or *immoral* acts. Honor crimes, rapes, molestation, and any other charges filed against a woman's honor are listed as immoral acts.

Using the above numbers, it's easy to see that far more than twenty-five women are murdered each year for reasons of honor. It's also obvious that the official numbers report only a small percentage of honor crimes. The government has chosen secrecy, rather than face the embarrassment of such large numbers. Also, if the real numbers were known and published, the government would be under greater pressure from Western governments and human rights organizations to stop these crimes. As it stands, the Jordanian government can pretend it hardly ever happens, and so can the Western governments reluctant to intervene in other nations' cultural practices.

In 1998, the U.N. conservatively estimated that over 5,000 women are killed for reasons of honor every year, 1,000 of those in Pakistan and Afghanistan, around 400 in Yemen, 50 in Lebanon, 1000 in Egypt, and the rest, about 2,550, in the West Bank, Gaza, and Jordan. Considering the fact that Jordanian population is larger than populations of the West Bank and Gaza combined, it's easy to conclude that the majority of these 2,550 lived in Jordan.

Two articles in Jordan's Penal Code allow these murders and protect the murderers. Article 340 exempts from punishment those who kill female relatives found committing adultery, and reduces the penalty for those who kill female relatives found in a *situation* of adultery (such as talking to a stranger). Article 98 reduces the penalty for the perpetrator of a crime when he acts "in a fit of fury" in response to a wrongful and serious act on the part of the victim. The mere rumor or suspicion that a woman has acted immorally is considered a wrongful and serious act on the part of the victim, and all perpetrators of honor crimes claim to have acted "in a fit of fury." These laws give men the freedom to kill their female relatives even when they only suspect immoral behavior. Most men turn themselves in to the police immediately after killing a female relative and are bailed out by family members while awaiting trial, and the time they spend out on bail counts as time served once they're convicted. Men who are not fortunate enough to be bailed out, normally because they don't have the money for bail, usually spend less than three months in prison and are treated as gods while they're there. Since honor killing is considered a misdemeanor, the offenders who are not released only receive short sentences, ranging anywhere from three months to two years.

But activism is beginning to unsettle things in Jordan, stirring the pot of frustrations. Current women's and human rights activists in Jordan are a mixed group—some foreigners, but most from the class of modern, educated Jordanians who have studied abroad. The ones who have found a means to "speak out" come mainly from very wealthy or powerful families. The issue is also getting the attention of many young university students. Most of the signatures on petitions to abolish laws protecting honor killings are those of university students, a promising sign that many of the younger, educated Jordanians want to see this practice outlawed.

According to activists currently struggling to abolish Article 340, most victims are innocent women. Most of the honor killings are based on suspicion and rumor and are often committed for financial reasons, i.e., inheritance. Activists have called these crimes a basic violation of human rights and have been trying to abolish the laws that permit their practice since 1998. Officials and medical examiners have confirmed that approximately 90 percent of honor crime victims had not engaged in any sexual activity, or were innocent of the acts they were rumored to have committed. These crimes do not receive international attention, though one woman reporter at the *Jordan Times*, an English-language weekly paper printed in Jordan, made a brave stance against these primitive customs, in the face of threats on her life, and began reporting on the crimes in the early nineties. Her reports have been chilling, and reveal that honor crimes are on the rise.

In August 1997, His Royal Highness Crown Prince Hassan—in an effort to bring attention to the crime—stated that honor crimes top the list of murders committed in Jordan. Originally it was believed that if the crimes were published it would cause them to decrease in number by frightening women into submission. Since these crimes have started to be publicized, there have been several reactions. Many women, as well as some men, have been outraged, though not shocked, and have begun to demand either the abolition or amendment of Articles 340 and 98. The issue created a prolonged period of public debate in 1998, and a draft calling for their abolition was finally submitted to the National Assembly. Royalty joined this abolition effort when, that year, the Jordanian National Commission for Women, chaired by HRH Princess Basma, proposed to parliament a draft law that would cancel and replace the articles. Parallel to that proposal was a campaign organized by a group of eleven Jordanians that gathered over 15,000 signatures on 713 petitions calling for the abolition of the articles, as well as any other legislation found to discriminate against women.

King Abdullah stood as an ally of women, publicly announcing that women's groups and women's rights organizations had his full support in the matter, and he told Prime Minister Abdur Ra-uf S. Rawabdeh to amend all laws that "discriminate against women and inflict injustice on them." The National Assembly opposed the draft, not once but twice.

The draft was destined to be defeated since the Islamic Action Front (IAF) holds the majority of the seats in the Lower House and they publicly oppose either abolishing or amending both Article 340 and Article 98, claiming that the Council of Ministers was seeking to corrupt public morals and impose Western values on Jordan's conservative culture in order to appease international human rights organizations. The Secretary General of the IAF, Abdul Latif Arabiyat, charged that the people leading these reform campaigns were trying to demoralize Jordanian society, and that the West was using the women's issue to push Arab women to abandon their honor and values and to start acting like animals.

So much for Jordan's democratic system, or the decent efforts of the royal family, when faced with the will of parliament. The royal family, specifically the king and queen, are mainly public showpieces. Their job is to portray an image of modernity for the country, and they do their job quite brilliantly. Both Queen Raina and the queen mother, Queen Noor, have shown leadership; Queen Noor has sponsored several handcraft training centers and shops to help bring some financial independence to women. But the impact on women's rights is very limited. They really have no effect on the laws in the country. It is parliament that controls them, and the majority of parliament members are firm Muslims, strict believers in the ancient codes.

In August 1999, the same year that the draft to cancel Article 340 was rejected by the National Assembly for the second time, it was Arabiyat who called for change when the issue concerned economic reform. He accused the "influential forces in Jordan" of being hostile to democracy and freedom and of trying to protect their own interests. By doing so, he left the impression that any change to the laws that govern women, or to the laws that restrain women's rights, would be detrimental to the moral fabric of

Jordanian society, while change in every other area of government would be a step in the right direction.

The history of women's rights in Jordan is far richer than in many other Arab countries, but then most other Arab countries are not trying to call themselves democracies. The Jordanian National Assembly tries to ignore the fact that in order to achieve a democratic society, its governing body must be capable of liberalism. Though all members of the royal family, including King Abdullah, have publicly voiced their disapproval and disgust for crimes of honor, the National Assembly, which claims to be the voice of the people but is actually the voice of men, continues to oppose any amendments to Jordan's penal code that would protect women.

In November 2000, twenty countries, including Jordan, abstained from signing a United Nations draft resolution condemning crimes of honor. The U.N. General Assembly had called for the elimination of all forms of violence and crimes against women, and the draft resolution reaffirms that all forms of violence against women constitute grave violations of women's and girls' rights. Distressingly, the permanent representative of Jordan, His Royal Highness Prince Zeid Ben Raad, tried to have the word "premeditated" inserted before the words "crimes of honor." However, this would have defeated the entire purpose of the resolution, since most "honor crimes" are supposedly committed "in a fit of fury." Had they succeeded in modifying the wording of the draft, they would have signed the draft, while knowing that it would not curb the practice it was meant to stop.

❧

Over the past fifteen years Jordan has found itself in a paradoxical bind. In its efforts to attract foreign aid, foreign business investments, and tourism, it has struggled to present itself as a modern, liberal, and democratic society by publicly granting women certain freedoms. Jordan is known as one of the least oppressive Muslim countries and was among the first of these nations to give women the right to vote. Women are, by law, permitted to receive an education, drive, and work, and the National Assembly is now considering allowing them to get passports and travel without written permission from the most senior male of the family. But for most Jordanian women, little has changed. The "law" of the male members of their families does not allow them to enjoy many of these freedoms, and so all these "changes" and "modernizations" are purely cosmetic.

Injustices toward women are apparent in all spheres of Jordanian life, including its citizenship laws, child custody laws, family inheritance laws, divorces, and physical and psychological abuse. Women in Jordan live under an umbrella of fear since the daily possibility of violent death hangs, literally, as a sword over their heads. Yet these injustices continue to go unnoticed by the international community. Generations of women, both young and old, continue to suffer in silence.

The number of honor crimes in Jordan is on the rise, which is not surprising since women have been placed in an impossible catch-22. As the government tells them that they have increasing freedoms, women come to believe they have the right to express their views, to work, to drive, and to get an education. But if they attempt to act on any of these "rights," they find themselves in mortal danger if these "rights" violate their family's wishes. With unemployment high, many women are forced to find jobs, which sounds like a good thing. But with Arab men's ways of thinking, even taking up one of the acceptable types of jobs—nursing, for example—invites an attack on nurses as "whores" for touching or seeing men who are not fully dressed. With a penal code that protects and encourages men to commit honor crimes, many innocent women—led to the slaughter by promises of freedom—are killed by men who are still hailed as heroes for upholding their family's honor.

The struggle for women's rights and freedoms in Jordan may take a generation or more, as women have to battle against centuries of male patriarchy to break the chains that bind them. Even as the world enters a new century, Jordan's National Assembly, along with the governments of most Arab countries, still celebrate and protect a stubborn, outdated, male-chauvinistic attitude toward women and women's rights. As recently as August 2001, a former Jordanian Minister of Justice, Abdul Karim Dughmi, responded to a question about honor killings in the case of rape with a smile and the statement: "All women killed in cases of honor are prostitutes. I believe prostitutes deserve to die."

FAREWELL

*F*rom the distance of many thousands of miles and of different cultures, I can now see how long it will take to change such old beliefs. I feel the imprint of the past in my own mind and body as I struggle to live the liberated life I'm now free to enjoy. As I speak out from abroad, adding my voice to the fight for Jordanian women, I am still, personally, fighting the taboos taught to all of us from birth in an Arabic culture.

I still hear the same whispers from the desert that my brothers hear. The voices of my mother and aunts still haunt me, saying over and over as they did throughout my childhood, "A woman is like a cup; if someone drinks from it, no one will want it . . . A woman is like a sheet of glass; once it is broken it can never be fixed." When I see people on the street free and open with their affections, holding hands, hugging and kissing, I catch myself thinking it is wrong and shameful. And yet I yearn to be that free, and to feel comfortable with it. The man in my life tells me that it is sad that I was taught to have such negative feelings about something so beautiful, but in the Arabic culture love is not associated with anything beautiful; it is a means of control. It is part of the cultural and emotional baggage I will carry for a long time.

In retrospect, also, it seems so easy to see the mistakes you've made, all the details you were blinded to as you were actually living through them. Now I sit for hours thinking of such moments, saying "if we had," "we should have," or "we could have," and wondering if Dalia would still be alive if we'd done things differently. I can now see that our naïveté, our emotions, our idealism led us on a doomed path. After years of beating myself up for her loss, I believe that even if we'd made different choices, chances are very high that our secret would eventually have been discovered. I've realized, too, that as long as honor killing is allowed in Jordan, no woman is safe.

Thousands of women are being legally murdered every year, for reasons that would be unheard of in Western countries. Losing my soul sister to such a barbaric practice angered me and hurt me, but eventually it fueled me with the courage to put pen to paper and expose these archaic traditions. During the preparation of this manuscript, I have relived all of these moments, and I know that I will continue to remember, love, and cherish the short time that Dalia was part of my life. She was a truly remarkable woman, more courageous than I could ever hope to be. She had the courage to follow her heart, and live her beliefs. She paid for chasing her hope of freedom with her life. She was murdered for the most innocent and universal impulse—wanting to love and be loved.

I'd always believed that we'd spend our lives together, imagining us as neighbors and best friends raising our children together, cooking our dinners together. I never dreamed that my time with her would be cut short, or that my life would be a journey down this path, but I realize that she left me with a mission. It's a task I must undertake, a goal I pray to reach. I must find a way to expose honor crimes for what they truly are: legalized murder; to break through the official Jordanian code of silence and find a way to make all Arab women's silent cries for justice and freedom heard around the world.

My fight will have to continue being waged far away from Jordan. I still have a Jordanian passport, so, officially, I could return. I long to see my mother. But, if I went home, I fully believe my father and brothers would have no hesitation in carrying out my honor killing. They repeated their mantra to me, over and over, after Dalia's death, *"If you have a rotten apple in the bunch, take it out before it spoils the rest."* Dalia, to them, was a rotten apple, and they took her out before she could tarnish the rest of their reputations. Even if I were to return to Jordan a virgin, I have disgraced my family by running away. I have shown disrespect for them, and their rules. They would have to kill me to save self-respect; have to take out the rotten apple in their own family.

※

As a dissident émigré, I made Greece my home for several years, and, today—in another country I cannot divulge—most of my friends are Greeks, not Jordanians, for I am still afraid to have Arabic friends who may oppose what I'm doing. It has been difficult to make my way; in Greece I worked odd and hard jobs for very little pay, most of what I earned going to pay my expenses at an Internet café so that I could use a computer to write this book. I've set new goals, and would like to return to school and study law, something I had always wanted to do. It would now give me better tools to avenge Dalia, as I vowed to do the day she died.

This book is my start. I realize that my words alone will not change what is happening, but I hope they will bring light to what has been shrouded in mystery and darkness for centuries. I hope, by expanding the work of activists in Jordan who are constantly frustrated and supressed, it can be a positive next step toward abolishing these crimes. Michael, who has left the military but is still in Jordan, is active in this work, helping other women, putting himself at great risk. He will always remain my ally in this struggle, and I owe him more than I can say in words. And I pray that whoever reads this book, and hears the words I have been able to find, will voice their outrage, as I have here.

ℝ

The following are just a handful of the honor crimes that were recently committed in Jordan. They were all reported in the *Jordan Times* by the highly credible woman journalist who has courageously made this her cause. I've listed a few stories to show that honor crimes are not restricted to a specific age group, religious sect, or geographic region of the country. Honor-crime victims include women and young girls from all walks of life. The only thing that unites these women is the fact that a male family member murdered all of them.

One day in May 1994, Kifaya, a sixteen-year-old Jordanian girl, was strapped to a chair by her thirty-two-year-old brother, who gave her a glass of water, told her to recite an Islamic prayer, and slashed her throat. He then ran out into the street waving the bloodied knife and shouting, "I have killed my sister to cleanse my honor." His sister had been raped by one of her other brothers.

In October 1998, Khadijeh, a twenty-year-old Jordanian woman, ran away from home and was reported missing by her family. The police found her a week later and sent her for an examination to determine whether she was still a virgin, a standard procedure in missing persons cases. She was found to be a virgin and released into her father's custody. He took her to a deserted area, stabbed her four times in the chest, and slit her throat. He then turned himself in to the police still holding the knife, which he said he had used to kill his daughter and cleanse his honor.

Lina, a twenty-year-old Jordanian girl, became pregnant after being raped by her neighbor. When her pregnancy became apparent to her family, they decided to kill her. On September 24, her brother drove her to a nearby football field owned by the Jordan Phosphate Mines Company, parked the car, and asked her to get out. He then repeatedly struck her on the head with a rock, drew a knife, slashed her throat and her stomach, left her by the side of the road, and went to turn himself in. His family treated him like a hero and later bailed him out, bringing a white stallion for him to ride home. He was sentenced to three months in jail, but was instantly released because he'd served that amount of time waiting for the trial, even though he was out on bail the entire time.

That same month, a forty-three-year-old man killed two of his sisters. Kifaya, twenty-three, was shot twice in the back of the head and Nadia, thirty-two, was shot five times in the head and chest. Both were killed in their home in Amman because he suspected them of immoral behavior. According to a woman in the neighborhood, who wanted to remain anonymous, Nadia and Kifaya had good reputations, while their brother had a criminal record. Another neighbor reported that he might have killed his sisters because he didn't want them to inherit any property or money.

In June 1996, a twenty-seven-year-old man spotted his twenty-five-year-old sister, Nofah, with two female friends in Liayali Zaman Restaurant and Nightclub. He forcibly dragged her from the table and shot her seven times in the head and chest, causing a panic in the restaurant. Then he waited for the police to arrive and turned himself in, claiming he had killed her to cleanse his family's honor.

In March 1997, a man killed his fifteen-year-old daughter by crushing her head with a large stone because he suspected her of having had relations with a neighbor. He told the police that when he questioned her about the matter, she denied having an immoral relationship with anyone, but he later killed her because he didn't believe her. The forensic examination concluded that she'd never had sexual relations.

Also in March of that same year, a twenty-five-year-old, married, pregnant woman living in Irbid was shot to death by her brother. The family had discovered that she'd had relations with her husband prior to their wedding and urged their son to kill his married sister to cleanse their honor. She'd been married for three months and was two months pregnant.

In June 1997, a thirty-four-year-old Egyptian national raped an eighteen-year-old Jordanian girl. As is the law, both parties were placed in detention at Qafqafa prison to protect their lives. The governor forced the man to marry his victim, which was his punishment for the rape. Two weeks after the incident they were released from the detention facility. Later her father gunned them down, claiming that he had killed them to cleanse his family's honor and because he and and his family blamed her for the rape since she knew the Egyptian, who was a worker in the neighborhood.

In September 1995, eighteen-year-old Subhieh defied her uncle's wishes and married twenty-one-year-old Mohammed, the man she loved. Two weeks after they married, her fifteen-year-old brother, under instructions from her uncle, went to her home after her husband left for work and shot her five times in the head and chest. He immediately turned himself in, claiming to have cleansed his family's honor.

A fourteen-year-old girl was at home, talking on the phone, one day in February 2000, when her thirteen-year-old brother strangled her with the phone cord. The youth confessed to murdering her and told police that it was a crime of honor because she was talking to men over the phone.

Dalia's death never reached the newspapers.

DEDICATION

My dear Dalia, in your life you made me laugh and made me cry. You managed to touch my soul and become part of me forever, and in your death you've become my purpose for living. I write this book in loving memory of you, and I pray that God keeps you safe and happy until we meet again. Till then, *ya gazalle*, I know your spirit strengthens me, and your memory comforts me, and you will always remain a special part of my life.